To Dad
Merry
Christmas;
1986

love, Alex

Norfolk

**A TRICENTENNIAL
PICTORIAL HISTORY**

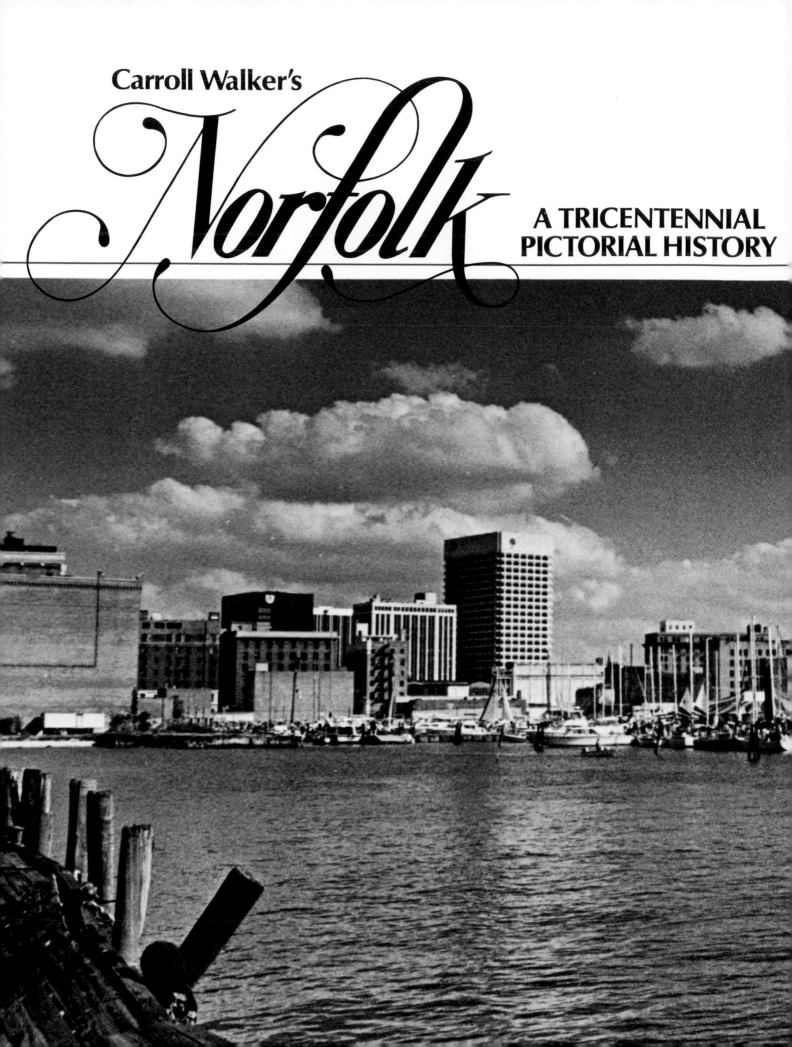

Carroll Walker's

Norfolk

A TRICENTENNIAL PICTORIAL HISTORY

Design by Jamie Backus Raynor

Donning Company/Publishers, Virginia Beach/Norfolk

Library of Congress Cataloging in Publication Data

Main entry under title:

Norfolk: a tricentennial pictorial history.

  Bibliography: p.
  Includes index.
  1. Norfolk, Va.—History—Pictorial works.
  2. Norfolk, Va.—Description—Views.   I.
Walker, Carroll, 1904-
F234.N8N88 1980   975.5′521   80-39668
ISBN 0-89865-129-8 (pbk.)   AACR1
Printed in the United States of America

Contents

For
Isabella
Carroll Theresa
and
Skip

Foreword

In September of 1975, a historic event occurred in the city of Norfolk: Carroll Walker published *Norfolk: A Pictorial History*. For over forty years, Mr. Walker has been collecting, identifying and restoring photographs on the city. With infinite patience and perseverence, he has been (and still is) saving photographs from oblivion; and with the publication of a book, he is ensuring that they will be available and accessible for generations. It has been my experience that few people realize the importance and significance of such work. There are of course many tens of thousands of photographs taken by and for the citizens of any city, but only a small percentage are relevant to documenting the city's evolution and growth. By thus collecting these disparate elements, Mr. Walker has helped preserve a vital record of a city and a society.

The problem with a book, however, is that there is a limit to the number of illustrations you can print. There must have been considerable pain and difficulty for Mr. Walker in culling his extensive collection for the 1975 book. Every photograph has a story: how it came to be taken, what is in it, how it was found. To Mr. Walker, who collects each with such loving care, it must have been akin to separating out children for a picnic. There were so many left behind. Thus, in honor of Norfolk's 300th anniversary, Mr. Walker has given the city another gift: *Norfolk: A Tricentennial Pictorial History*. In a whole new collection, filled with the anecdotes and lore only Mr. Walker could contribute, another valuable addition to the city's history is herewith presented.

We can only hope that other cities and towns have individuals like Carroll Walker, who make it possible for the rest of us to learn about and to appreciate our heritage. We are certain that with the publication of this volume, as well as the earlier work, Mr. Walker's own place in Norfolk's history will be secure.

Robert S. Friedman

Preface

This book, like its predecessor, *Norfolk: A Pictorial History*, published in 1975, is a continuing photographic history of Norfolk's past and present, with a minimum of words, letting the pictures speak for themselves, which they can do most eloquently. Since the publication of the 1975 volume, many more pictures have been found, and they have been used to fill in the spaces of a vast mosaic of Norfolk's past from which they have been missing for so long a time. They give a clearer and more comprehensive picture of the city's "yesterday." Such pictures were not necessarily taken by an outstanding professional photographer with the latest equipment of his or her time; they could have been taken by anyone with a simple box camera—a "Kodak", as early cameras of any make were usually called—anyone who happened unknowingly to freeze a moment of life somewhere that no one had caught before. There are many such pictures in this book.

Continuing research has revealed that many photographs of Norfolk and its people have been irretrievably lost. Years ago, in one instance, a large collection of Harry C. Mann's pictures and plates were permitted to leave the city because of a possible lack of interest on the part of some to locate storage space for them. In other cases, photographs have been carelessly destroyed, lost, or thrown away because of a lack of interest or knowledge of what they represented.

On the other hand, many persons possessing old pictures have either given them to me outright or permitted me to use them. One such person had an old album with delightful pictures of the old Ghent Bridge, taken in 1903-04 from the top floor of a house on Mowbray Arch, and other pictures a well, some of which are reproduced here. Another person offered me a picture of, as she could only describe it, "an old time auto stuck in a muddy country road," which her husband would have thrown away. This picture turned out to be a 1916 Ford mired in mud on what later became Granby Street. Its locale was near the intersection of Willowwood Drive and Granby Street. It is a gem and is reproduced in this book.

The years speed by too quickly, rendering our memories of locations and events hazy, but a good photograph puts such occurrences into sharp focus again, "unfreezing" those moments of eternity. When Main and Granby streets were Norfolk's main thoroughfares, they were almost always filled with people, especially on Saturdays and "sale" days. As business became more concentrated on Granby Street after World War I, Main Street went into a slow decline, most of it disappearing after 1960. In 1977 the old Granby Street was converted to a mall. Early Main Street is hardly remembered, and the memory of Granby Street's crowds is growing misty. The blocks between Freemason Street and City Hall Avenue were perhaps the busiest with the center around Smith and Welton and College Place. Imagine this corner on a busy Saturday afternoon, especially near Christmas, with crowds hurrying about, packages in their arms, cars bumper to bumper in the center of the street and similarly parked on each side of the street. Such descriptions might seem somewhat exaggerated to a newcomer to Norfolk who arrived here after "The Mall," but any doubt will be quickly dispelled by a photograph.

There are also some excellent pictures of Church Street during the 1930s and '40s, which street is almost nonexistent today because of post-war changes. After World War II the city expanded and became ringed with new highways and shopping centers which siphoned off the trade that was once an integral part of downtown Norfolk.

In many instances efforts have been made to match old scenes with a present day picture of the same location, showing the contrast. Sometimes in comparisons of this kind proportions may not appear to correspond. This discrepancy is often due to the original vantage point having been altered or having disappeared, necessitating a shift in angle and distance. Also, differences in types of equipment must be considered. Although not a photograph but a watercolor sketch, Latrobe's view of Norfolk's waterfront in 1796 from the Smith's Point (Botetourt Street) area offered an unobstructed picture of his subject. We could not repeat this same scene today because of the intervening piers and warehouses that have been built in the area over the years. However, a camera with a 28 mm. wide angle lens and a closer vantage point clear of any obstruction enabled me to photograph the same area as it appears today, making possible an interesting comparison of the two scenes.

The response to *Norfolk: A Pictorial History* was very gratifying. I received letters from former Norfolkians from all over the country, expressing in many ways their pleasure in possessing such a book. And many persons new to Norfolk felt that it gave them a better visual picture of the city and its past. It is hoped that this book will be as well received.

As with the first book, it was difficult to make a satisfactory selection of pictures for this one, having again to go through the torturous task of eliminating excellent pictures because of space limitations. The work of both professional and nonprofessional photographers has supplied many a missing piece to the grand historical mosaic of Norfolk, and that's what makes the task so interesting.

Last but not least, I again express my sincere appreciation to those whose names appear with the captions under the many pictures in this book as well as those with whom I have discussed Norfolk's past, present, and future, some of whom, regretfully, passed away before this book was written.

I do wish, however, to make some special mention of a few:

Lucille Portlock and Peggy Haile of the Kirn Memorial Library's Sargent Room for their invaluable assistance in helping me locate missing bits and pieces of Norfolk's historical mosaic.

Betty Williams, who thoughtfully saved that picture of "the old time car stuck in the mud" on Indian Pole Bridge Road (Granby Street)—a priceless conversation piece.

Grover Franklin and Curtis Mills of the city Survey Office, who "straightened" me out on many a crooked street of yesteryear.

John Tadlock, for his racing pictures and stories about automobile racing.

Ben Leon, who sold me my first long pants suit, for his stories about the Jamestown Jockey Club race track on Hampton Boulevard. He was almost arrested the afternoon the track was raided on the governor's orders. (He thought they were taking movies.)

William Steinhilber, for stories about the racing crowd, the track, and the Monticello Hotel, headquarters of the Jamestown Jockey Club.

J. Burnell Bragg, a youngster at the time of the races. His father was appointed special prosecutor by Governor Stuart to break up gambling at the track. His father received so many threats that he sent his family away, and while they were gone, someone burned his house down.

Ira White, One of the last "survivors" of the "famed" Norfolk Light Artillery Blues polo team, organized in 1924. This was one of the first polo teams in the world to use croquet mallets with broom handles.

Mrs. Hunter Savage, whose thoughtfulness in giving me those small pictures found in an old album of the Ghent Bridge and area taken from the top floor of a house on Mowbray Arch in 1903-04 is most appreciated.

Mrs. Allen Peltz, who now owns the house on Mowbray Arch from which the pictures mentioned above were taken and who permitted me to take matching pictures from the same room.

George Holbert Tucker, who always has a tale or two about old Norfolk whether it is good or bad. When it is good it is interesting and when it is bad it is hilarious!

John Parker, general reference, Kirn Memorial Library, whose cooperation has been excellent.

James Sweeney, archivist, Old Dominion University, and Dr. Peter Stewart, professor of history at ODU.

Donna Reiss Friedman, for her excellent suggestions and help in editing the text and picture captions in this book.

And there are many others whose names are not on picture credits, such as George Curtis, Richard Ruffin, Arthur Polizos Associates, Helen Shober, Judy Baroody, and Larry Maddry.

And I must not forget my dear wife, Isabella, whose patience has been beyond words and who waited hopefully for the day when she again could see the top of the dining room table.

Introduction

As Norfolk approaches its 300th anniversary, the words of the poet James Russell Lowell come to mind:

O visionary world, condition strange,
Where naught abiding is but only Change.

To have lived in Norfolk since the beginning of World War II is to have witnessed a change that is mind-boggling. Since its birth in 1680, Norfolk's growth has been slow and irregular. Although the town was first surveyed in 1680, no lots were sold until 1683 when a Peter Smith bought three. A few years later, in 1687, six more lots were sold. But it was not until 1691 that the town began to grow when the Assembly ordered the separation of Lower Norfolk County into Norfolk and Princess Anne counties and the construction of a new courthouse and other buildings. By 1700 a few hundred people were living here, and by 1775 Norfolk had a population of 6,000. It was considered the most prosperous town in the Virginia Colony, and its future appeared to be assured.

Unfortunately, Norfolk's fortunes changed. It was totally destroyed during the Revolution. After the war, a rapid recovery seemed on its way, made possible by the beginning of the Napoleonic wars in Europe in 1792. However, the Embargo Act of 1807 and the subsequent War of 1812 dashed any hopes of Norfolk's regaining her former position. Nor did the building of the Erie Canal in 1826, attracting traffic through the port of New York and highlighting the lack of a railroad at Norfolk, help. The Norfolk and Petersburg Railroad (now the Norfolk and Western Railway) did not begin operating until 1858.

The yellow fever epidemic of 1855 was a setback to the city, and a few years after came the War Between the States. Although the city suffered no physical damage during the war, its progress was stifled not only for the duration of that conflict, but during the Reconstruction period, which ended in 1871. While the city was in a bad state, financially and otherwise, its recovery was fairly rapid. One significant change was the beginning of its first streetcar line in 1869.

Because of a lack of public transportation, Norfolk's population had always lived within the confines of a semi-circle of less than a mile from the center of the city, Market Square (Commercial Place).

When the first horsecar arrived in Norfolk in 1869, it operated first on Main Street, and then it began to extend its service to other sections of the city, enabling people for the first time to break out of their boundary. When the system became electrified in 1894, the outward movement became further accelerated.

Another change that affected the city's growth was the filling in of Towne Back Creek to Granby Street. The creek originally extended to "the Road that Leadeth to the Woods," now St. Paul Boulevard. In 1796 a visiting architect, Benjamin Henry Latrobe, described it as "a creek navigable for boats at high tide into the heart of the town." The creek lost most of its navigability when in 1818 the town authorized the construction of a stone bridge across the creek at Granby Street, and the extension of Granby Street from the bridge to Main Street, joining the two streets together. This part of Granby Street was new.

In 1898 on the northwest corner of City Hall Avenue and Granby Street were a few wooden buildings extending to what became Brooke Avenue. With the exception of the Monticello Hotel, which was built that year, there was no other business activity on Granby Street, only stately homes with gardens and high brick walls. But when the Monticello Hotel opened in September 1898 for the first time, it was like a starter's gun at a race track. Almost immediately old structures came down as new construction raced up Granby Street, and in ten years time it had changed from a quiet residential street to a busy commercial thoroughfare. The old homes were replaced by office buildings, theatres, hotels, and shops of all kinds.

Other changes were taking place at the same time as new suburbs came into existence, such as Ghent, Colonial Place, Park Place, Larchmont, Edgewater, Lochaven, Algonquin Park, Winona, and Ballentine Place. By 1911 Norfolk's population had jumped to 76,671.

But another event was taking place that would change Norfolk's future—World War I. Overnight the city expanded in all directions. In 1917 the old Jamestown Exposition site was acquired by the Navy and the construction of the Naval Base began. Near Sewell's Point a huge Army Base went up. Workers swarmed in from all over the country and supplies and equipment moved through the port as did hundreds of thousands of servicemen. Unfortunately, the city quickly became overcrowded, causing unjust criticism. The city's efforts to alleviate this condition were unavailing; the sudden expansion and overcrowding were too sudden.

With the war over in 1918, the city returned to normalcy. Growth continued, and in 1923 Norfolk annexed twenty-seven square miles of territory and about 30,000 additional people. This included the Army Base, Naval Base, Ocean View, and some other suburbs. Ever changing, the city grew, adding new schools, new industry, a new market building, and an airport in 1938.

Perhaps Norfolk's greatest change came with World War II. After the fall of France in 1940 the government began the enlargement of the Naval Base, extending it to Granby Street. Once again, hordes of workers poured into the city, creating overcrowding conditions almost immediately. With our entry into the war in December 1941 and the increased influx of workers, servicemen, and their families, the overcrowding became critical, although new housing developments were going up everywhere in an attempt to alleviate the situation.

After the war, and unlike 1918, Norfolk was experiencing a slight boom. It needed more land. On January 1, 1955, the Tanner's Creek District was annexed, and on January 1, 1959, a part of Princess Anne County was taken in.

Growth and change continued. On May 23, 1952, a bridge-tunnel to Portsmouth was opened, eliminating the ferries that had operated for almost two centuries. In 1963 another tunnel was opened from the foot of Hampton Boulevard to Pinner's Point in Portsmouth. In 1957 a bridge-tunnel was opened from Willoughby Spit to Old Point Comfort.

In 1951 the city began a slum clearance project involving some of the worst sections of the city. The first was an area off Monticello and Brambleton avenues, finished in 1954 and named Young Park after one of Norfolk's distinguished citizens, P. B. Young, Jr.; another such project finished in 1955 was

called Tidewater Park. A new wholesale and manufacturing area called the Industrial Park was created on the site of Broad Creek Village on Virginia Beach Boulevard.

Numerous other developments were taking place in the 1950s. But the biggest project of them all was the remodeling of 140 acres in the heart of downtown Norfolk, eliminating the old beer taverns and flophouses on East Main Street, a growing eyesore, as well as the other sleazy-looking buildings in the area, and replacing them with new buildings and streets. The work of demolition began in July 1958. Many new buildings were erected, the largest of them all being the Virginia National Bank at the head of old Commercial Place (which was eliminated forever) and Main Street.

During this period a new convention center called Scope was built. Adjoining it is Chrysler Hall, home for many theatrical and musical performances. The Norfolk Museum of Arts and Sciences became the Chrysler Museum, housing the magnificent collection of Walter P. Chrysler, Jr. A new Civic Center was created in the area of old Church and Main streets, in which are located the courts buildings, City Hall and jail, as well as new office buildings. A new hotel, the Omni International, covers the area where ferries used to dock at the foot of Commercial Place. And plans for the further development of the Towne Point area are in the offing.

The old Southgate Terminal area is being completely renovated; docks are being repaired and made available for watercraft once more. College Place has been extended to Botetourt Street and townhouses erected. The old Monticello Hotel has come down and a new structure, the Federal Building, has been erected in its place. And many other changes have taken place in Norfolk. The city's future looks bright.

And so, as we face the future, we wonder what old Peter Smith, the purchaser of the first three lots in Norfolk Towne in 1683, would say were it possible for him to return here. After looking around, he might take his cue from a cigarette billboard and say, "You've come a long way, baby!"

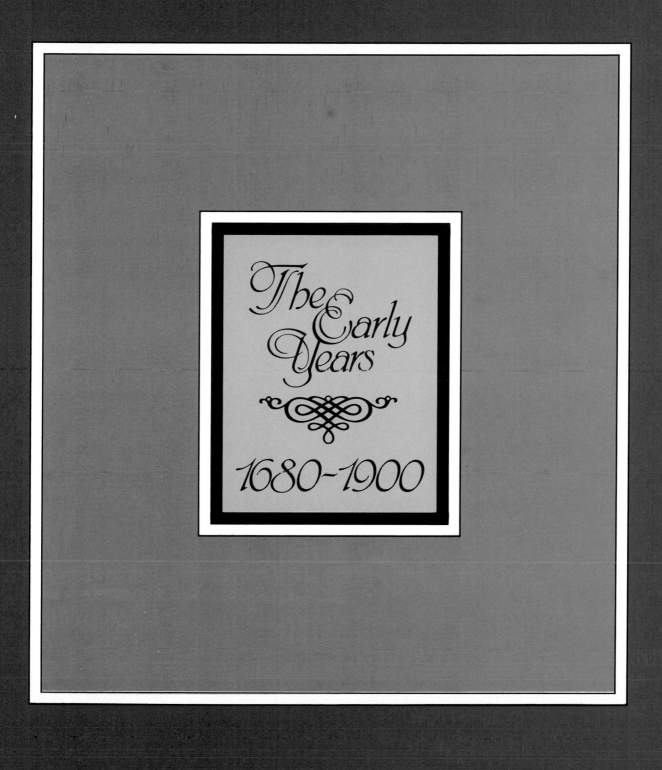

The Early Years

1680~1900

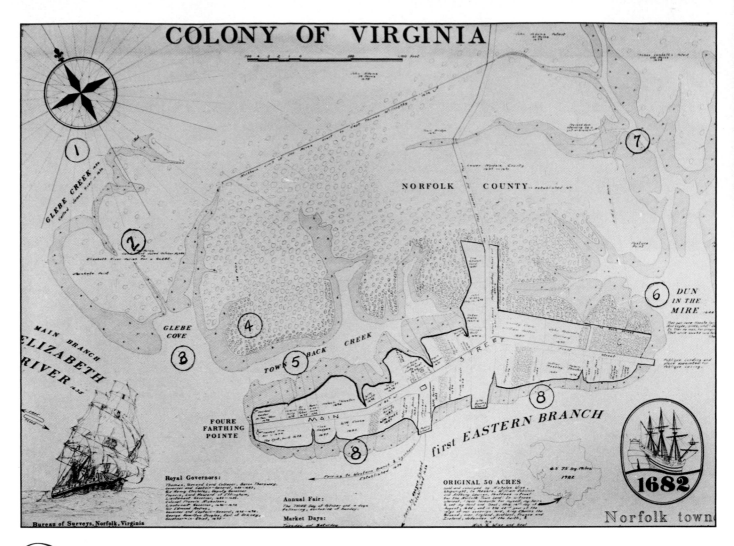

COLONY OF VIRGINIA

NORFOLK COUNTY

DUN IN THE MIRE

first EASTERN BRANCH

Norfolk town

1682

Bureau of Surveys, Norfolk, Virginia

Royal Governors:

Annual Fair:

Market Days:

ORIGINAL 50 ACRES

$\mathscr{I}$n 1872 a balloonist, flying high above
Norfolk, observed from his balloon that
"Norfolk appeared to be an island surrounded by
a network of rivers...." To confirm this statement,
consult any old map and see, as someone once said,
"what a soggy place old Norfolk was" when it was
selected for the townsite in 1680. Original old Norfolk
was virtually an island, connected to the mainland by a
narrow umbilical cord. All around were coves, creeks,
and inlets that poked their watery fingers deep into the
irregular shoreline, creating small and large patches of
marshland; but much of this has disappeared, having
been filled in over the centuries. Vestiges still remain,
however, in the form of the Lafayette River (once
known as Tanner's Creek) and the Hague, one branch
of which extended northwardly beyond Twenty-First
Street and another branch eastwardly to Church
Street. And the filling-in still goes on.

Grover Franklin and Lionel P. Brown of the
Bureau of Surveys, Norfolk, have compiled and drawn
a map (reproduced here) of the area after it was
surveyed in 1680-81 by John Ferebee, county survey-
or. A commentary on the map follows.

(1) *Glebe Creek* was the name first given to the
body of water later to be known as the Hague. The
eastern branch had several names: Smith's
Creek, Paradise Creek, Puddin' Creek (some
say it was "Puttin" Creek), and lastly the Hague.
The other arm of it was known as Colley's Creek,
named after John Colley, whose home was on a point
just east of present day Colley Avenue and Brambe-
ton Avenue. Upper and lower Stockley Gardens are
located on the site of the creek.

(2) To the south of Glebe Creek was a land grant
dated October 30, 1686, to the Elizabeth River Parish
for a Glebe (usually a plot of land granted to a
clergyman as a part of his benefice during his tenure of
office). It was sold by the vestry of St. Paul's Church on
January 14, 1734, to Samuel Smith, a merchant. This
area became known as Smith's Point, and the creek,
Smith's Creek. In this general area lie the streets
Botetourt, Dunmore, Yarmouth, and Duke, running
north and south, and the western part of York, Bute,
and Freemason streets. College Place, which extends
westwardly from Granby Street, originally ended at
Duke Street, but as the area beyond was filled in, it has
been extended, ultimately to Botetourt Street in 1974.
College Place was originally known as Green Bush
Street, then Washington Street, and when the Norfolk
College for Young Ladies was built in 1880 on the

corner of Washington and Granby streets, the name was changed to College Place. One finger of Glebe Creek from the north almost reached Bute Street. All of those indentations have since disappeared.

Smith's Creek extended eastwardly to Church Street, crossing James Street (now Monticello Avenue) at Ninth Street where a bridge stood known as Armistead's Bridge. This creek also separated the two cemeteries, Elmwood and Cedar Grove. Along the west boundary of Cedar Grove Cemetery, a finger of the creek extended almost to Twenty-First Street. In 1912 drainage work began on the creek in this area, converting it into dry land. A stone bridge at Duke Street near Olney Road crossed another finger of the creek. A part of the bridge's stone railing was still standing as late as 1946.

(3) Glebe Cove has disappeared entirely. At one time a finger of it extended across Knight Street (Freemason Street) between Botetourt and Dunmore streets while another finger extended northeastward across Freemason and Yarmouth streets.

(4) Much of the shoreline area and slight indentations here have been reclaimed and filled in. The Southgate Terminal complex and a part of the Free-mason Harbor development area are now located here.

(5) Towne Back Creek originally extended east-wardly almost to old Church Street (the "Road that Leadeth out of Town")—now St. Paul Boulevard. In 1833 the Virginia General Assembly authorized "the course of Cove Street altered [now City Hall Avenue] and the Back Creek above Bank Street filled up, and a suitable public square created." In 1840 the water was dammed out from the space between Granby and Bank streets. The square was subsequently estab-lished and became the site of the 1850 Courthouse (now the MacArthur Memorial). By 1884 it was completely filled in to Granby Street, becoming City Hall Avenue in 1884. The rest of the creek west of Granby Street to Boush Street was filled in by 1905 and Boush Street extended to Main Street, eliminating a short street known as Newton Street. One long finger of the creek extended north across Freemason Street near Granby. When this was filled in, Tripoli Street, named after Stephen Decatur, was created between Courtenay (Tazewell) Street and Wolfe (Market) Street. In the 1890s a new street was planned to run from Tripoli Street to meet with James Street at Bute Street. When this was done, Monticello Avenue came into existence, eliminating both Tripoli and James streets.

A few other small fingers of Towne Back Creek cut into the shoreline. One ran northward to Wolfe (Market) Street between Catherine (Bank) Street and Cumberland Street. On the opposite side running south, one finger almost reached Commerce Street at Main Street and the other extended along Talbot Street almost to Main Street. This would be on the side

of the waterfalls next to the United Virginia Bank Building.

(6) On the east side of Church Street was a large creek originally called Dun-in-the-Mire, which later became Newton's Creek. After 1865 it was known as Mahone's Lake, named after General William Ma-hone, C.S.A., builder and president of the Norfolk and Petersburg Railroad, predecessor of the Norfolk and Western Railway. As the creek was gradually filled in, the reclaimed land was used as storage yards for the Norfolk and Western Railway, the Norfolk Southern Railroad, and the Virginian Railway. In 1912 an eight-story railroad office and passenger station building was erected at the end of East Main Street on the filled-in land.

(7) At one time a long finger of Newton's Creek extended northward to the Virginia Beach Boulevard-N&W Railway crossing on the latter's Lambert's Point Branch. And in 1761 a finger of the creek extended northwestward to Charlotte and Church streets where it was crossed by a bridge known as the Towne Bridge.

(8) As one can readily see, the original area of Norfolk was not very long nor was it very wide, in some instances only a few hundred yards or less in width. The shaded area around the original fifty acres laid out for Norfolk Towne provides a very good idea of how much land was reclaimed and developed. Water Street, for example, located between Main Street and the river, was Norfolk's wholesale and manufacturing area until about 1950, when its decline accelerated. Research seems to indicate that it was some kind of a street along the water's edge from which there were piers and docks and that it did not actually come in existence as a street until after the Revolution; that in 1782 "Cornelius Calvert, George Kelly, Cary H. Hansford, Joel Mohun and John Woodside were appointed a committee to survey and lay off 'a Water Street,'" which they did, and their plan was approved. The street was created by filling in from the then-existing shoreline to the Port Warden's Line, using ship's ballast, sand, logs, shells, and heavy refuse.

Unfortunately, the street lived up to its watery name, for during northeast storms or any disturbances that created unusually high tides, the street flooded quickly, causing a cessation of business to a greater or lesser degree to all business along the street and some side streets running down to the water.

A few years ago, when the city was digging up City Hall Avenue preparatory to laying a new box culvert, the first in almost a century, it was interesting to note the large quantities of oyster shells that had been used in the original fill. Oyster shells were very plentiful in this area and had a wide and varied use, not only as a general fill material, but also for fertilizer (crushed oyster shell lime), aggregate in concrete, and road building. They are all over the city. And as one man said: "The people of Norfolk were raised on oysters and the city built on oyster shells."

Norfolk is believed to be the only city in the United States possessing a silver mace which has come down from colonial days. At one time a mace, possibly developed from a crude club, was definitely a weapon of war used largely by military leaders, and thus it evolved into a symbol of authority.

The mace was presented to the Borough of Norfolk in 1754 by Robert Dinwiddie (1693-1770), lieutenant governor of Virginia from 1751 to 1758. It was made in London of pure silver. Although an inscription upon it states it was given to the Corporation of Norfolk in 1753, records indicate that Dinwiddie delivered the mace in person in 1754.

When Norfolk was burned on January 1, 1776, the Mace was removed to Kemp's Landing (now Kempsville) for safekeeping and later returned to Norfolk.

In Norfolk's earlier days the Mace was always carried ahead of the mayor upon his entering court or before him in processions. On the one hundredth anniversary of Norfolk as a borough on September 19, 1836, it was carried in a parade.

When Norfolk was evacuated by the Confederates on May 10, 1862, the Mace was hidden by Mayor William W. Lamb under a hearth in his home on West Bute Street. For some reason or other, the whereabouts of the Mace seem to have been forgotten until it was found in 1894 in bad shape in an old record room at the police station.

The Mace has been carefully restored and is now in the custody of the Virginia National Bank, where it is displayed in an especially built glass case in the main office of the bank downtown.

Much reference is made in early Norfolk history to Town Back Creek, a large body of water that once extended almost to Church Street (St. Paul Boulevard) and to the Stone Bridge, built in 1818, that joined upper and lower Granby streets.

This picture shows the bridge and creek as they looked to a local artist around 1845. According to a local historian of the 1890s—Thomas Rowland—it was done from a filled-in area that became Bank Street. It was further filled in to Granby Street by 1884, becoming City Hall Avenue, and extended to Boush Street by 1905.

Granby Street was named after the Marquis of Granby and came into existence about 1762. It originally extended from Bute Street to the creek, a wooden bridge connecting it to a Concord Street on the other side since lower Granby Street did not then exist. In 1818 the city authorized the construction of a stone bridge across the creek and the extension of a new street to be called Granby a little west of Concord, which still exists today as a lane running alongside the Trailways Bus Line.

The dark line extending from the bridge to the center is Granby Street. The wall is that of the Tazewell Estate, which was taken down piece by piece in 1903 and replaced in Edgewater. The small buildings on the right are on the Dickson property.

Today the old Royster Building stands a little to the right of the stone bridge. The Monticello Hotel was on the center right where the Dickson home was; the new Federal Building now stands there. Courtesy of Emily Derrickson

In 1938 Charles Morrisette, a Norfolk artist, made this painting of the presentation of the Norfolk Mace to the Corporation of Norfolk by Robert Dinwiddie, Governor of Virginia, on April 1, 1754. It is not known what has become of the painting, and it is quite possible that it is the only one of its kind ever made.

When Benjamin Henry Latrobe (1764-1820), who was to become the architect of the U.S. Capitol and the "first great civil engineer in the United States," visited Norfolk in 1796, he made a watercolor of Norfolk's then existing waterfront, titling the picture "View of Norfolk from Towne Point" as shown here. This would roughly cover the area from Towne Point to present-day City Hall Avenue. It is felt that Latrobe meant a view of Towne Point and that he made his sketch from a location on the end of Smith's Point, possibly in the vicinity of Botetourt or Freemason streets. This would have given him the sweeping view he painted. Smith's Point was opposite Towne Point and was in general the terminal area of York, Bute, Freemason, and Botetourt streets west of Boush Street. This area was once a part of the glebe lands of old St. Paul's Church and was acquired by a Samuel Smith in 1734, hence the name Smith's Point.

On the left of Latrobe's picture are two needle-like objects jutting above the skyline. Latrobe referred to the first as the location of "the new courthouse" (Nebraska Street) and the second as the "old courthouse in the Marketplace now converted into stores." This would have been Commercial Place near the corner of Talbot and Main streets. Also under the second "needle" he refers to a body of water as "a navigable creek for boats at high tide into the heart of the town." This would be Town Back Creek, now City Hall Avenue. In the center of the picture was the Customs House on the corner of present day Randolph and Main streets. The other buildings, such as wharves and warehouses, were located on what was Water Street, now Waterfront Drive, where ships are anchored. Latrobe also refers to the "small town of Gosport" on the extreme right as being divided "from Portsmouth by a small creek navigable by the tide."

This picture was made twenty years after Norfolk was totally destroyed and is possibly the earliest known illustration of Norfolk. It clearly shows the rapid progress Norfolk was making in rebuilding the town. Courtesy the Papers of Benjamin Henry Latrobe, Maryland Historical Society

An effort has been made here to compare the present waterfront area from Towne Point to City Hall Avenue with Latrobe's view in 1796. Of course, with the changes that have been wrought on the waterfront in 300 years, that is, the construction of piers, warehouses, buildings, the filling in of much of the shoreline, extending it in many instances, it was not possible to get the same view from where Latrobe stood. However, this general view of the present Town Point area was obtained from another site which compares favorably with Latrobe's view. With the exception of the remains of the old Anheuser-Busch Brewery building on the extreme left, the original part of which was built on reclaimed marsh land of Back Creek (now City Hall Avenue), which Latrobe referred to as "the creek navigable,"—the area in question has been completely cleared of buildings and piers. In its heyday, the area bustled with activity, being the terminus for several boat lines maintaining regular freight and passenger service north. The cluster of tall buildings in the center is located in Norfolk's downtown financial district. The tallest building, the Virginia National Bank, located on old Commercial Place, dominates the area. Photograph by Carroll Walker, 1980

There are very few people living today who will remember the beautiful residence of George Newton that once stood on the southwest corner of College Place and Granby Street. The house was built on what was once a part of the original Boush estate. It was conveyed in 1801 by Conway Whittle to a Thomas Willing, who in turn conveyed the lot for the sum of one dollar to the Bank of the United States at Norfolk, whom he represented, on March 25, 1802. Immediate construction of a building was begun, and on September 7, 1803, the bank opened for business in this building. This is regarded as Norfolk's first and only bank at the time. Two brick guardhouses for sentries were placed on each side of the bank as shown in this 1893 picture.

The bank functioned until 1811, when the charter of the Bank of the United States, granted by Congress in 1791 for twenty years, expired and was not renewed because of the strong opposition of state banking interests. Although its closing was a serious blow to the community, the property was acquired by the Farmers Bank of Virginia, with headquarters in Richmond, which occupied the building in 1812. Incidentally, in the early days bank buildings were constructed so as to provide a residence for the cashier or president and their families.

In 1826 the building was sold by the bank to George Newton, a member of one of Norfolk's leading families at that time and former mayor of the borough. The property remained in the Newton family until 1893, when it was sold to J. Wesley Fentress, a prominent Norfolk businessman, who remodeled the building for commercial purposes. In addition to offices, the Norfolk Library Association and its successor, the Norfolk Public Library, had rooms in the building until their new quarters were ready in 1903 on Freemason Street. In 1897 the first Christian Science meeting was held in Norfolk in this building. In 1910 the old home was torn down to make way for a four-story building. Photograph courtesy of Kirn Memorial Library

This picture by Harry C. Mann shows the decline of the George Newton home. It was announced in the Virginian-Pilot for July 10, 1910, that the house was to be taken down and a new structure erected in its place.

The building that was erected on the site of the old Newton home and completed about 1912 has had many and varied occupants. Some years ago Fine's Clothing located their store on the corner of College Place and Granby Street. The building was recently renovated, as shown in this 1980 picture. Photograph by Carroll Walker

Sometime in 1812 Charles Lee built a home on a part of the old Llewellyn tract in present-day East Ghent, given to him by his father-in-law, Abel Llewellyn. Although situated less than a mile from the downtown Norfolk of that time, it was considered very much "out in the country."

Over the years Norfolk grew, and in 1845 it was designated as a city. However, it was not until 1890 that its expansion accelerated with the development of Ghent. After 1900 the old farmland in the East Ghent area began to disappear as the laying out of streets started and new houses made their appearance. The old Llewellyn-Lee home was designated as being on the northwest corner of Fourteenth Street and Omohundro Avenue.

Charles Lee's descendants continued to live in the house until 1928, when they moved to another location but still retained ownership of the house. It was rented out until sometime in the 1960s, when the housing authority acquired it. Although all houses in the area were taken down, his house remained standing, boarded up and unoccupied. It was offered for sale—for $1.00—to anyone who would remove it from the property. *Courtesy of Robert Sutton*

In 1981 the Lee-Llewellyn house was purchased by Phyllis Brown, who had the house removed from its original location to another site on Llewellyn Avenue, just a few blocks away and still on the original tract. With a few alterations on the front and an addition to the rear, the house has otherwise been faithfully restored. *Photographs by Carroll Walker*

21

Few people who come down to the end of Bolling Avenue in Edgewater to watch the boats pass by or the sun go down, are aware of the fact that Craney Island, across the river from Edgewater, was once the scene of a short but terrific battle that saved Norfolk from destruction a second time, on June 23, 1813.

Aggravated by the defeat of their ships at sea, attacks on Canada, and the burning of their capitol at York (now Toronto), the British prepared to retaliate against the United States, and the Chesapeake Bay area in the early part of 1813 offered the most enticing target. The British declared both the Chesapeake and Delaware bays blockaded, and an expedition under Adm. J. B. Warren was organized at Bermuda, with Vice Adm. George Cockburn, a tough old sailor with a penchant for looting and destruction, second in command. In February 1813 lookouts at Cape Henry sighted British ships off the coast and immediately warned the military authorities in Norfolk.

Norfolk had long taken precautions for such an attack. It was protected by two small forts: Fort Norfolk at the foot of present-day Colley Avenue and Fort Nelson on the grounds of the future Naval Hospital. A string of gunboats stretched across the mouth of the Elizabeth River between Norfolk and Craney Island, where a strong force of infantry, artillery, and militia was stationed on the island. However, when the British fleet

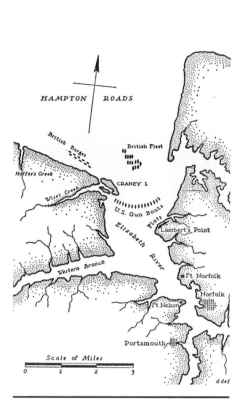

arrived in Norfolk, they considered Norfolk too strong at that time and turned to terrorizing the Lynnhaven and Chesapeake Bay areas as far north as Baltimore. This was a temporary relief for Norfolk.

The British under Admiral Warren returned to the area on June 1, 1813, with a large fleet and a landing force of 5,000 men, many of whom were veterans of Wellington's campaign in Europe. The American forces con-

sisted of several thousand men under command of Gen. Robert B. Taylor. General Taylor had placed a strong force consisting of two companies of artillerymen, a company of riflemen, militiamen, regulars, volunteers, and 150 sailors and marines from the Constellation, a total of 737 men, of whom many were veteran fighters. These forces were posted on the northeastern part of the island adjacent to the gunboats, a position of strategic importance. The British planned to engage the force in front while another force would land on the mainland, cross the shallow water on the left of the island, attack the American flank, and break the line of American gunboats.

The attack began on the morning of June 23, 1813. As 2,500 men landed to the west of the island, 50 barges containing 1,500 soldiers and marines left the fleet for the island, led by the big green barge of Admiral Warren. The Americans calmly awaited the approach of the British and when close enough the order to fire was given. The fire was devastating. One of the many barges hit was that of the admiral, and those that weren't sunk quickly returned to the protection of the fleet's guns. The attack on the flank was likewise unsuccessful, and when the British land forces saw what happened to the men in the barges, they also retreated, leaving the Americans in possession of the island and Norfolk safe from a sure destruction.

Craney Island from Bolling Avenue in Edgewater, Norfolk. Some American positions were located where the telegraph poles are in the center of the picture. It was from this part of the island that the British barges were

sunk. Other British forces landing on the mainland in the distance were repulsed when they attempted to cross the shallow water between the western shore and the American left flank on the island. Much of this area

has been filled in over the years, joining the island to the mainland. The "island" is now a naval activity. Photograph by Carroll Walker

Tucked away in a corner of Norfolk's west side at the intersection of Front Street and Colley Avenue in the Atlantic City section is Fort Norfolk, a small fort built in 1794 after the Revolution. The construction of the fort was ordered by President George Washington for the protection of Norfolk on 4½ acres. Fort Nelson, a similar fort, was built on the opposite side of the Elizabeth River near the Naval Hospital's present location. Inactivity in the fort brought it into a state of disrepair, but a threat of war in 1807 brought about a decision to repair it and Fort Nelson.

At the outset of the War of 1812, the fort was activated again. Local militiamen, U.S. Regulars, and some men from the U.S.S. Constellation composed its garrison when a British fleet on June 23, 1813, attempted to pass Craney Island and capture Norfolk. It is said that an impediment to this was a heavy chain stretched from Fort Norfolk to Fort Nelson possibly to stop the British fleet should Craney Island fall. However, as the British were decisively defeated at Craney Island and left the area, this proved unnecessary.

The fort again resumed its inactive

status until the War Between the States began. On April 19, 1861, Norfolk militia companies took possession of the fort for the Confederacy. It was retaken by Union forces under Gen. John Wool on May 10, 1862, without any action. In May 1863, the fort was transferred to the U.S. Navy by Gen. B. F. "Spoon" Butler,

who in turn transferred the various prisoners and stores. The fort was later reoccupied by the army.

In 1923 the Norfolk District, Corps of Engineers, occupied the fort, remaining in it until 1935, when it moved to the post office building. In 1942 it returned to the old fort. Photograph by Carroll Walker, 1981

This drawing of Fort Norfolk appeared in Harper's Weekly in 1861.

This aerial view of Fort Norfolk was taken in 1934. Courtesy of William Bradshaw, Jr.

On the southwest corner of the old W. T. Grant Company building on Market Street and Monticello Avenue is a metal plaque stating that the first Confederate flag flown in Norfolk was unfurled from a housetop about a block and a half east of this corner, April 2, 1861, two weeks before the secession of Virginia from the Union. There has always been some question why the plaque was not placed on the original building from which the flag flew. A story is told that the original building was on the northwest corner of Bank and Market streets, but because it had acquired in later years an unsavory reputation as a bawdy house, it was more appropriate to place the marker on a less notorious building. Photograph by Carroll Walker, 1980

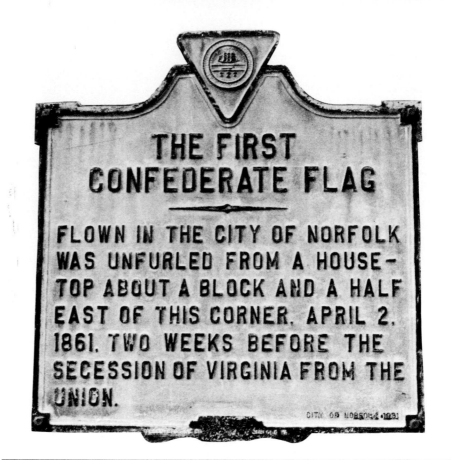

THE FIRST
CONFEDERATE FLAG

FLOWN IN THE CITY OF NORFOLK WAS UNFURLED FROM A HOUSE-TOP ABOUT A BLOCK AND A HALF EAST OF THIS CORNER. APRIL 2, 1861. TWO WEEKS BEFORE THE SECESSION OF VIRGINIA FROM THE UNION.

CITY OF NORFOLK 1931

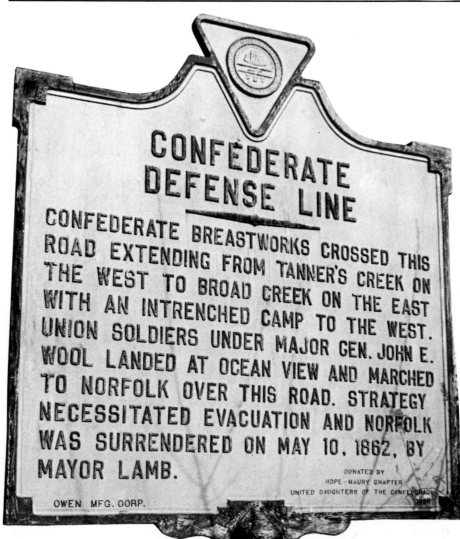

CONFEDERATE
DEFENSE LINE

CONFEDERATE BREASTWORKS CROSSED THIS ROAD EXTENDING FROM TANNER'S CREEK ON THE WEST TO BROAD CREEK ON THE EAST WITH AN INTRENCHED CAMP TO THE WEST. UNION SOLDIERS UNDER MAJOR GEN. JOHN E. WOOL LANDED AT OCEAN VIEW AND MARCHED TO NORFOLK OVER THIS ROAD. STRATEGY NECESSITATED EVACUATION AND NORFOLK WAS SURRENDERED ON MAY 10, 1862, BY MAYOR LAMB.

DONATED BY
HOPE-MAURY CHAPTER
UNITED DAUGHTERS OF THE CONFEDERACY

OWEN MFG. CORP.

When Virginia seceded from the Union in April 1861, preparations for Norfolk's defense were immediately begun. At that time the main road leading into Norfolk was Princess Anne Road, often referred to as the "County Road," which terminated at Church Street. A lesser road known as Sewell's Point Road (a part of which is now Little Creek Road) and ran northeasterly to Princess Anne Road at the present Industrial Park. Where Ward's Corner is today, Sewell's Point Road connected with a narrow country road running to the outskirts of Norfolk. It was known as Indian Pole Bridge Road and would later become Granby Street. This road crossed Tanner's Creek (now Lafayette River) over the Indian Pole Bridge (built about 1845) and connected with Church Street a mile distant. At that time Granby Street terminated at York Street.

Breastworks were built from Broad Creek through part of the future site of the Industrial Park, crossing Princess Anne Road and coming to rest on a point of land on Tanner's Creek about 100 yards from Ballentine School. Behind the breastworks were twenty-two cannon and a large concentration of Confederate soldiers from many parts of the south. The camp was known as the "Intrenched Camp." When Maj.-Gen. John E. Wool of the Union Army landed at Ocean View on May 10, 1862, he marched to Norfolk over the Indian Pole Bridge Road. He was stopped at Tanner's Creek because the Confederates had burned the bridge and were shelling him from a small battery on the south side. Wool had to retrace his steps to the Ward's Corner area and enter Norfolk over Princess Anne Road, passing through the breastworks and camp to Church Street where he received the surrender of the city. The camp had been evacuated by the city and the cannon rendered useless by spiking. While the breastworks were ultimately destroyed, a visible small part of them still existed on the point of land beyond the school as late as 1950. Many Ballentine school children in other years have found campsite artifacts in the area such as Minie balls, buttons, belt buckles, and swords. They were displayed in the Ballentine School for many years in a case which has long since disappeared.

This metal marker, showing the location of the city's defense line, was donated and erected by the Hope-Maury Chapter, Daughters of the Confederacy, in the 1960s. It is located on Princess Anne Road near the Ingleside Road across from the old Texaco office building. Photograph by Carroll Walker

The Colley-Mottu-Johnson House, shown in 1959, had been a residence, a hospital, a school, and a boarding house before it was torn down in 1961-62 to be replaced by the Pembroke Towers apartments. The house was built by John Colley sometime before 1850 on land between Smith's Creek (now the Hague) and Fort Norfolk Road (now Colley Avenue). During the Yellow Fever Plague of 1855 Colley and three of his children succumbed within a few weeks.

The house became a hospital when the Retreat for the Sick, established in 1883 on Holt Street in a Spanish-style house built in the 1870s, outgrew its quarters and moved into the old Colley residence in 1896. The name was changed to Protestant Hospital. In 1936 it became Norfolk General Hospital.

Eventually the house was acquired by J. Andre Mottu, Norfolk businessman and consul for the Netherlands, who had bought property in the newly developing Ghent area bounded roughly by Redgate, Thetford (later Hampton Boulevard), Raleigh, and Colley avenues. Because the hospital desired to expand and because Mottu wished to acquire their waterfront property, an exchange was arranged. Although the Ghent section was developing rapidly, Mottu turned his land into a veritable farm. The Netherlands flag always flew from a pole on his property.

During the 1920s the property changed hands again. At one time it was reported as being used temporarily as a boys' school, another time as a boarding house. About 1948 the house was purchased by Thomas G. Johnson, a businessman and sportsman who lived in it until 1961, when it was acquired by the Norfolk Redevelopment and Housing Authority. Photograph of house courtesy of Thomas G. Johnson; photograph of Pembroke Towers by Carroll Walker, 1980

On March 28, 1895, the Norfolk
Retreat for the Sick, graduated its first
nursing class. The hospital, located on
Holt Street at that time, was the
predecessor of the present Norfolk
General Hospital. Courtesy Southgate Leigh III

When William Mahone was twenty-seven years old, a graduate of the Virginia Military Academy, and a construction engineer by profession, he was chosen to be chief engineer of the newly planned Norfolk and Petersburg Railroad, the forerunner of the present-day Norfolk and Western Railway. This was to be a stretch of track eighty miles long from Petersburg to Norfolk, a portion of which would run through a dense, swampy area known as the Dismal Swamp, considered by many to be impassable. Despite all criticism, Mahone was successful, and in 1858 the first train moved into Norfolk.

When the War Between the States began in April 1861, Mahone was president of the Norfolk and Petersburg Railroad. The fate of the Gosport Navy Yard near Portsmouth was in the balance. Confederate troops were in possession of Norfolk and Portsmouth. Commodore McCauley, the Federal commander of the Navy Yard and apparently of a somewhat vacillating nature, had been called upon to surrender by Gen. William B. Taliaferro, who was then commanding the Confederate forces in the area.

Word had been received that some Union gunboats were moving up the river to destroy the drawbridge by which the railroad entered Norfolk.

Mahone quickly called for volunteers. With his master of transportation, Henry Fink (later to become president of the Norfolk and Western Railway), he loaded the volunteers on some flatcars and went out personally to defend the bridges, which he found safe. After going several miles beyond them, he saw no trace of the gunboats. Mahone, however, knew that the Union troops at the Navy Yard had received a report that Confed-

erate forces from Georgia and the Carolinas were on their way to capture the Union establishments. Mahone then adopted the ruse of having the engineer of the train run it back and forth several times across the bridge, blowing the whistle and ringing bells in such a manner as to give the impression that several trains, probably troop trains, were approaching. This was too much for Commodore McCauley, who fell for the deception; and rather than risk capture in the poorly defended port, he gave orders to destroy the yard, abandoning it that night. Fortunately, the dry dock was not destroyed. It fell to the Confederate forces without a shot being fired.

Nine days later Mahone was commissioned a lieutenant-colonel in the Confederate Army. A week later he was made a full colonel, commanding the 6th Virginia Regiment, which regiment was composed of more Norfolk men than any other outfit in the Confederate Army. After the Battle of the Crater at Petersburg in 1864, he was made a brigadier-general.

Mahone never wore the regulation Confederate uniform, preferring one of his own design, as shown in the picture. It was his opinion that uniforms were too uncomfortable.

The end of the War Between the States found the Norfolk and Petersburg Railroad in bad shape, and not until February 1866 was the road again open to traffic. President William Mahone succeeded in having a bill passed to merge the Norfolk and Petersburg Railroad, the Southside Railroad, and the Virginia and Tennessee Railroad into the Atlantic, Mississippi and Ohio Railroad which connected at Bristol, Virginia, with the East Tennessee and Georgia Railroad, giving Mahone a through route to Memphis, Tennessee, which he had long sought.

The picture of the locomotive shown here was typical of that used by the Atlantic, Mississippi and Ohio Railroad and was taken in Lynchburg around 1870. Although it was well known what the initials "AM&O"

stood for, the road was jocularly referred to as "All Mine and Otelia's," Otelia being the name of Mahone's

wife. The road became known as the Norfolk and Western Railway in the 1880s. Courtesy of Tal Carey

This is possibly one of the oldest photographs ever taken of Market Square (later Commercial Place). Its date would be in the 1870s. When Norfolk was surveyed and a few streets laid out in the fall of 1680, one such street running south from Main Street to the water was designated as "the street that leadth to the water's edge." After a market building was erected at the north end of this street in the early 1700s, it became known as Market Square and also as The Parade, a drill ground. About 1900 it became known as Commercial Place. At first, almost half of the length of Market Square was under water to Union Street but was subsequently filled in with ships' ballast and other materials, reaching its final length many years ago. After the market building at the head of the square was burned in the early 1800s, a new building was erected on reclaimed land closer to the water and the ferries. A concrete pad extended northward from the building, as shown in this picture, on which farmers erected temporary open stalls for the selling of their produce and other items. About 1892 a new market was erected on City Hall Avenue to which farmers then brought their produce. But Commercial Place still remained a lively, busy place until the ferries stopped running in 1954, resulting in pedestrian and vehicular traffic by-passing the area. The end came in the early 1960s as the city moved to demolish the area. Courtesy of Cook Collection, Valentine Museum

Sometime around 1875 George Cook, a Richmond photographer, recently of Charleston, South Carolina, took a picture of Norfolk's waterfront, covering the area from the tip of Towne Point (right) to about where City Hall Avenue is today. This may be the oldest known photograph of Norfolk's waterfront. The steamer on the left is on the Norfolk-Boston run of the Merchants and Miners Transportation Company. The white vessel is one of the Old Bay Line steamers running between Norfolk and Balti-more. Between the two vessels can be seen the spire of St. Mary's Catholic Church on Holt Street and the dome of the Courthouse. The square structure above the steamer is the top of a cotton compress near Newton (later Boush) and Plume streets. The cotton merchants were located in this area and along the waterfront to Mathews Street (Towne Point) before they moved to the Atlantic City section of Norfolk in the late 1890s. The dark-roofed building in front of the white square-rigger is the Atlantic Hotel on Granby and Main streets. The low, white, many-windowed building in the center is the Customs House. Courtesy of Cook Collection, Valentine Museum

The later picture is the identical area as it appeared in 1979 and still looks in 1981. The piers and ware-houses have all disappeared and present plans call for the construction of new buildings a little right of center as well as a further renovation of the waterfront. Photograph by Carroll Walker

This is a rare picture taken about 1895 of six survivors of the C.S.S. Virginia (Merrimac). Among them are James E. Barry, who commanded the first railway mounted gun used in warfare and the battle of Savage's Station near Richmond in 1862, and Thomas Keville and A. J. Dalton, volunteers of the Merrimac during its first engagement with the federal fleet in Hampton Roads on March 8 and 9, 1862.

Left to right, standing: Capt.

Thomas Keville of the United Artillery, Norfolk; H. B. Oliver, gunner, C. S. Navy; former U.S. Navy 1st Lt. James E. Barry, United Artillery, Norfolk. Seated: William Jarvis, carpenter's mate, C. S. Navy; E. V. White, engineer, C. S. Navy; C. J. Creekmur, engineer yeoman, C. S. Navy; Andrew Dalton, United Artillery, Norfolk. Courtesy of Old Dominion University Archives

This building at the corner of Main and Granby streets may possibly be the oldest existing structure on Granby Street. It is believed to have been built the latter part of the 1860s to house the S. A. Stevens Furniture Company, formerly located on Main Street near Church Street. In the late 1890s Stevens Furniture went out of business, and the building was taken over by Watt, Rettew and Clay, generally known as Watt's, a prominent dry goods and millinery store. Watt's succumbed to the Depression about 1930. The building was later occupied by the Willis Furniture Company and then the Haynes Furniture Company, which moved away in the 1960s, and the building is now vacant.

The name Thomas Godwin and Company (also operating as the Virginia Iron Works) may not be familiar to many present-day Norfolkians, but for years this concern manufactured locomotives for narrow gauge railroads and others, such as lumber companies, at their plant on Water Street. They began business around 1868 and ceased operations in 1924. Two photographs of their products appear in this book: the locomotive shown in this picture was built for the Norfolk and Virginia Beach Railroad Company in 1884 and was named the Jas. W. Hopkins. The other locomotive appears in the section about Ocean View, Photograph courtesy of Janet F. Taylor

Ocean View

The March 1, 1855, issue of the Southern Argus, a newspaper published in Norfolk, announced the formation of the Ocean View Company, which had purchased ten acres of waterfront property for the purpose of erecting a private summer resort. Construction began almost immediately. Slowed down during the War Between the States, its popularity began to grow after the conflict ended. It was reported that people stopping in the area on their way to Florida were so pleased with the climate they preferred to remain here. This picture of Ocean View dated 1878 shows the beach and a few houses. Courtesy of Kirn Memorial Library

The resort remained somewhat static until 1879, when the first railroad to Ocean View was built. This was the Norfolk and Ocean View Railroad Company, a narrow-gauge, single-track affair. For several years the equipment consisted of one small toy-like locomotive, pictured here, and three open-type cars. The locomotive, named for Col. Walter H. Taylor (inset), president of the line and former adjutant-general to Gen. Robert E. Lee, was built in the Norfolk shops of Thomas W. Godwin and Company. For many years this miniature locomotive was the sole motive power, sometimes handling ten or twelve cars loaded with passengers. Some years later, as the popularity of the resort increased, another engine was added, named for John B. Whitehead, mayor of Norfolk from 1874 to 1876.

Many years ago Colonel Taylor wrote an account of the experience of going to Ocean View in the early 1890s when the terminus of the railroad was on Henry Street, near Princess Anne Road and Church Street. Getting to Henry Street was an ordeal in itself; going to Ocean View was another. Sunday was the big day: trains left daily at 10:30 a.m., 3:00 p.m., and 5:30 p.m.

Colonel Taylor states that "the three o'clock train was the most popular...often every car was pressed into service to handle the crowd. Often flat cars, such as are now used for handling sand from the beach [probably low-sided gondolas] were requisitioned. Wide, thick boards, laid across the sides of these served as seats. So anxious were the pleasure-seekers to reach the seashore that the younger element, in particular, did not mind sitting in the broiling sun for an hour, sometimes longer, while the puffing and wheezing locomotive struggled along the eight miles or so, hauling as many as fifteen cars at times."

In the late 1890s the road was electrified, enabling it to offer better service and more scheduled trains and increasing the attendance at Ocean View. About the same time the Ocean View Hotel was built. Courtesy of Janet F. Taylor

Otto Wells was soon joined by his brother, Jake, and Ocean View began to surge ahead with new amusements, fishing, boating, and bathing as well as easy access from Norfolk. Excursion trains from the interior brought more people, many of whom had never seen a body of water as large as the Chesapeake Bay, or as one old "Ocean Viewite" said, "never saw so much salty water in their whole life." One enterprising man sold souvenir bottles of "real ocean salt water" for five cents. This view shows the popularity of the resort beach on July 4, 1930.

In 1904 Otto Wells, an amusement entrepreneur from Richmond, Virginia, became interested in Ocean View, saw its possibilities, and took over the amusements from the railroad. This postcard view dated 1905 shows a pavilion and a "Leap-the-Dips," as roller coasters were called in this area. Fishing boats are shown on the beach. Courtesy of Norfolk Historical Society

In the early 1900s a large, beautiful ballroom was built and later attracted many "big bands" such as Guy Lombardo and Paul Whiteman. In 1928 a Spanish-type hotel, the Nansemond, was built, and during World War II the North African invasion was planned there. The hotel burned in 1980.

Over the years the amusement park has endured some exciting moments, including fires in 1911 and 1914, the latter destroying most of the old "Leap-the-Dips." In 1958 fire destroyed the old ballroom, which was never rebuilt. There were also severe storms. A northeast gale in 1921 did heavy damage, and the 1933 hurricane wrought extensive damage. During the hurricane a flagpole sitter, who had climbed the pole July 4 with a vow to remain until Labor Day, refused to come down. When the fire department could not bring her down, a professional climber brought her down safely.

This circa-1955 aerial shows calm weather at Ocean View before the season opened. Courtesy of Norfolk Historical Society

After World War II the Ocean View amusement park area began a slow decline. Although fishing remained popular, it was not enough to sustain the resort area.

The finale for Ocean View amusement park was grand: a motion picture company, learning of the planned disposal of the park, arranged to explode the old "Leap-the-Dips" in a movie. Here crowds gather in the summer of 1979 as the coaster is prepared for demolition. The man at upper left stands in readiness with a fire extinguisher. Photograph by Carroll Walker

The "Leap-the-Dips" resisted the first attempt to bring it down. It was still standing after the explosion. Another attempt a few days later was more successful, perhaps because of the assistance of a bulldozer. Photograph by Mort Fryman, August 27, 1979

A resort since 1855 and an amusement park since 1900—in 1979 the end of an era. Photograph by Carroll Walker

An architect's rendering of a possible plan for the site of the former Ocean View amusement park. Courtesy of Communications and Marketing Division, Norfolk

A difference of one hundred years is shown in the time intervening between the taking of these two pictures. The inset picture shows the old wooden footbridge, known as the Drummond Bridge, that connected Botetourt Street with the present day Ghent area in 1880. It was also known as the Drummond farm. In the center of the picture is the Drummond farmhouse.

The modern view shows the same area as it looks in 1981. The development of Ghent began in 1890, and it grew rapidly. About 1894 the wooden bridge was replaced by a more modern structure over which streetcars ran. This was replaced in the 1970s by a smaller metal footbridge. The Holland apartments at the foot of the bridge were built in 1905 on the site of the old Drummond house. The body of water in the foreground was originally known as the Glebe Creek, Smith's Creek, Puddin' Creek, Paradise Creek, and after 1900 as the Hague. It was bulkheaded with stone in the early 1900s. The area gets its name from Ghent, Belgium, where the 1815 treaty of peace ending the War of 1812 between Great Britain and the United States was signed. Inset courtesy Kirn Memorial Library; photograph by Carroll Walker

At the Peoples Cheap Hat Store, operated by Lloyd T. Reed at 101 Church Street in 1890, Mr. Reed stands in the doorway. The derbies worn by the two men were high fashion at the turn of the century. In 1910 there were ten hat stores operating in Norfolk. All of them invariably sold nothing but men's hats. Courtesy of Elizabeth Cofer

The Centenary Methodist Church, built in 1889, originally stood on the corner of Boush and Queen (later Brambleton Avenue) streets. About 1911 the congregation moved to the corner of sixteenth Street and Colonial Avenue, becoming the Colonial Avenue Methodist Church. The church on Boush Street was taken over by a black congregation in 1912 and the church renamed the Jerusalem Baptist Church, operating until about 1949. The church was taken down in the late '50s. Photograph by H. D. Vollmer; courtesy of Kirn Memorial Library

In the late 1950s the Home Federal Savings and Loan Association acquired the old Jerusalem Baptist Church and erected in its place this building. Photograph by Carroll Walker, 1980

This was the reception area of William Freeman's studio as it appeared in 1892. He opened his studio in 1888 at 208½ Main Street, near Church Street (St. Paul Boulevard) and later moved to 176 Main Street when he took a partner, John H. White. The partnership was later dissolved, and by 1917 Mr. Freeman had given up his photographic business and had opened a book and stationery store on Granby Street. Courtesy of Kirn Memorial Library

The Spanish cruiser Reina Mercedes in drydock at the Norfolk Navy Yard. The Reina Mercedes was sunk at Santiago, Cuba, on July 8, 1898, during the Spanish-American War, then raised and brought to Norfolk for overhauling and repairs. She was later used as a station and receiving ship at Annapolis, Maryland, retaining her Spanish name. In the early part of September 1939 she was towed to the Norfolk Navy Yard for general overhauling. When the work was completed, she returned to her station at Annapolis. Courtesy of Kirn Memorial Library

This was Botetourt Street just below Freemason Street in 1895. On the left can be seen a part of the old Selden House. On the opposite corner a little to right of center was the home of Col. Charles R. Grandy. Courtesy of Kirn Memorial Library

This is the same Botetourt Street shown in the 1895 picture as it looks in 1980. While both the Selden and Grandy homes are still standing, many other changes have been made. Where Botetourt Street was a dead end at the waterside originally, the area has been filled in, and it now connects with extended College Place. New townhouses stand where a house had stood in the 1895 picture. Photograph by Carroll Walker

This is the 1891 senior class of the Norfolk College for Young Ladies. The college was located on the northwest corner of College Place and Granby Street, built about 1880 and closed in 1900. The structure later became the Algonquin Hotel. The street gets its name from the school. The building still stands, the top boarded up and the bottom converted to stores. Courtesy of Old Dominion University Archives

This early northeasterly view of Norfolk was taken from the Atlantic Hotel on the corner of Granby and Main streets about 1897. The two most prominent buildings in the picture are the City Market (also known as the Armory) on the left center, built in 1892, and the Courthouse (now the MacArthur Memorial) built in 1850, on Bank Street. Plume Street is shown in the center; the buildings in the lower left are on Plume and Granby streets. They would be mostly destroyed in the Atlantic Hotel fire of 1902. The trees in the lower right are on Concord Street, a very narrow street (we would call it an alley today) that existed before lower Granby Street and was connected by a wooden bridge with upper Granby Street. Concord Street extended from Back Town Creek to Main Street. It now exists as a lane next to the Trailways Bus Station. The lower part of Granby Street was created when a stone bridge replaced the wooden structure over the creek in 1818. Courtesy of Old Dominion University Archives

The general area around Church and Union streets was the center of the livery stable business. One such firm engaged in this business was that of Hannan and Kelly, located at 40-44 Union Street and also at 64 Church Street, whose business was probably the largest of its kind. Taken about 1893, this picture shows their operation on Union Street. They handled all classes of animals, from the common dray horse to the best roadsters and trotters. Their sales averaged about $200,000 yearly. They began operations in 1872 and closed in 1915. *Courtesy of Kirn Memorial Library*

The White and Dodson Hardware Company was located on the corner of Main Street and Commercial Place. They represented the Cleveland Bicycle Company (address unknown). The man on the cycle is Joe Grimes, a heavyweight pushing the scales at 570 pounds. As a promotional stunt for advertising the bicycles, Ira White, Sr., had the company send Grimes to Norfolk to demonstrate the strength of their product. Special size seats and pedals were provided, but the other parts were all standard, such parts being readily available. In this picture, circa 1895, Ira White is seemingly trying to hold Grimes up. *Courtesy of Ira White, Jr.*

Anyone for biking? These young ladies have taken to the countryside (or a nearby park) in the latest cycling style of 1897—leg-of-mutton sleeves and Dad's Homburg hat. The young man in the center seems to be the happiest in the crowd. *Photograph by Walter H. Taylor III; courtesy of Janet F. Taylor.*

One of the many manufacturers along Water Street, Norfolk's wholesale and manufacturing area, was the Eagle Foundry, established in 1886 and out-of-business after World War I. Note the different size propellers made by this concern. The picture was taken in 1893. Courtesy of Kirn Memorial Library

An early Norfolk brewery was the Consumers Brewing Company located at 729 Church Street, organized in 1895. Taken in 1896, this picture shows the brewery and one of its delivery trucks and teams of horses. It ceased to operate when Virginia went dry in November 1916. An unsuccessful attempt was made to market a fruit juice drink during the early days of Prohibition, and the plant remained closed until the repeal of Prohibition in 1934 when it resumed operations under the name of the Southern Breweries. The plant is now operated by the Champale Products Company. Courtesy of Kirn Memorial Library

Another firm doing business on Roanoke Dock was W. M. Cook and Company, handling hay, grain, and mill feed. It was established in 1869. The picture was taken in 1893. Courtesy of Kirn Memorial Library

The City National Bank, built in 1895 (picture 1896) occupied the northeast corner of Main and Atlantic streets. It was taken over by the National Bank of Commerce in the next block of Main Street, the building taken down and a new one erected on the site about 1905. In the early 1960s the name was changed to the Virginia National Bank when a new twenty-three-story building was erected on the upper part of Commercial Place and Main Street. The older building was taken over by the First and Merchants National Bank.

A 1980 photo of the First and Merchants National Bank on the northeast corner of Main and Bank streets. When the National Bank of Commerce changed its name to the Virginia National Bank and moved into the new building across the street, the First and Merchants National Bank acquired the old building. Photograph by Carroll Walker

The Henry Walke Company, mill and steamboat supplies, began business in 1884. This picture was taken about 1896 when the Walke Company was located on Commerce and Water streets. Next to it in this picture was the wholesale hardware firm of Watters and Martin, which began operations in 1866. Both firms are still in business, having moved some years ago to the Norfolk Industrial Park. Courtesy of Kirn Memorial Library

Monticello Hotel

When the Monticello Hotel opened on September 27, 1898, it was considered one of the finest hotels in the state. At the time it was built, City Hall Avenue was comparatively new, being shown in the city directory for the first time in 1885. Originally the site of a creek extending almost to Church Street (St. Paul Boulevard), it finally had been filled in to Granby Street. With the exception of a few small buildings on the west side of Granby Street from City Hall Avenue to Brooke Avenue (also new), the rest of Granby Street northward was lined with lovely homes. But once the hotel opened, the street was transformed overnight to a burst of building activity, and in a few years the homes gave way to stores.

The hotel endured for seventy six years through fire and flood, so to speak. During its life it saw Norfolk grow and change. It was always the center of social and political activity downtown. After a disastrous fire in 1918, two extra stories were added, containing a large dining room and a horseshoe-shaped ballroom, known later as the "Starlight Room," a favorite place for dances and balls. During World War II it served as a nightclub. This photograph was made shortly after the hotel opened. Courtesy of Mrs. Armand Vipond

On the morning of January 1, 1918, the Monticello Hotel caught fire and was totally destroyed. The weather had been bitterly cold for weeks, and on the day before the fire, December 31, 1917, the temperature registered a high of 16 degrees and a low of 9 degrees Fahrenheit. Water directed to the building froze immediately. A ladder on the City Hall Avenue side was frozen to the building for several days. For years this picture was a favorite on postcards. Photograph by Harry C. Mann

The hotel was rebuilt after the fire and reopened early in 1919. While at first there was a question as to whether the hotel could be rebuilt because of the war and the scarcity of structural steel, the government, realizing the need for hotel accommodations in Norfolk, gave permission to the contractors to provide the steel. The lobby of the rebuilt hotel is shown in 1919. Courtesy of Kirn Memorial Library

Col. Charles H. Consolvo had been connected with the hotel since 1905 and was president of the corporation when the hotel burned. He saw that no expense was spared to make the new Monticello the best in the state—which it was. Courtesy of Kirn Memorial Library

On August 23, 1933, Norfolk was suddenly hit by a devastating hurricane. The water rose so high it was impossible to get in or out of the Monticello Hotel at either its City Hall Avenue or Granby Street entrances. This group of youngsters are in front of the Monticello Hotel's Granby Street entrance. Several of them had been diving off the tops of the cars. Courtesy of Kirn Memorial Library

After many years of distinguished service to the public and a gradual change in the downtown area after World War II, the use of the hotel declined, occasioned in particular by the movement of business from the area and the emergence of motels on the periphery of the city. Attempts at renovation failed.

About 1970 the hotel was sold, and a few years later it was decided to take it down and to erect in its place a new federal building. On January 26, 1976, the Loiseaux Company, professional demolitionists, prepared the hotel for its end. Here the Monticello begins its collapse. *Photograph by Sandy Grice from the Board of Trade Building*

Clouds of dust rise as the Monticello falls. As the dust slowly cleared, one onlooker was heard to say to a friend: "What tales those old walls could tell if they could talk!"

"Yes," replied the friend. "If those walls could talk, a lot of people would leave town." *Photograph by Carroll Walker*

What took more than a year to build in 1918-19 came down in 1976 in less than five seconds with the push of a plug. Photograph by Carroll Walker

The new Federal Building, completed in 1979, stands on the former site of the Monticello Hotel and the Dickson Building at Granby Mall and City Hall Avenue. The building on the right is the Maritime Tower. The Federal Building has received considerable local criticism, including the observation that it resembles the old tobacco warehouses in Richmond. Photograph by Carroll Walker

In its first 200 years, Norfolk had seen prosperity and disaster, and its growth had been slow and unsure. But as the twentieth century approached, the city seemed to be stirring, perhaps sensing it was on the threshhold of a new period.

When this 1892 "bird's-eye-view" of Norfolk and its environs was made, the city for all of its 200 years had spread very little beyond Smith's Creek on the north and Newton's Creek on the east as the map shows. Almost all of Town Back Creek (City Hall Avenue) had been filled in, and there were still some watery areas of Newton's Creek extant. Two bridges, the Norfolk and Western Railway and the Campostella (lower right) spanned the Eastern Branch of the Elizabeth River. The railroad's tracks had been extended in a wide sweep

around the city through farmland to its new coal pier at Lambert's Point (center left), paralleling today's Twenty First Street. Ghent (center left), started in 1890, was rapidly developing, and Brambleton (center right), dating from 1875, had already been annexed by the city in 1887. Almost everything beyond the dark center mass, as the map indicates, was farmland.

However, as Norfolk began to break out of its "cocoon" as it neared the turn of the twentieth century, it would expand rapidly, particularly as the country became engulfed in two world wars. Its boundaries would soon reach the Elizabeth River on the left and the Chesapeake Bay on the top, and it would continue easterly until stopped by the formation of the new city of Virginia Beach.

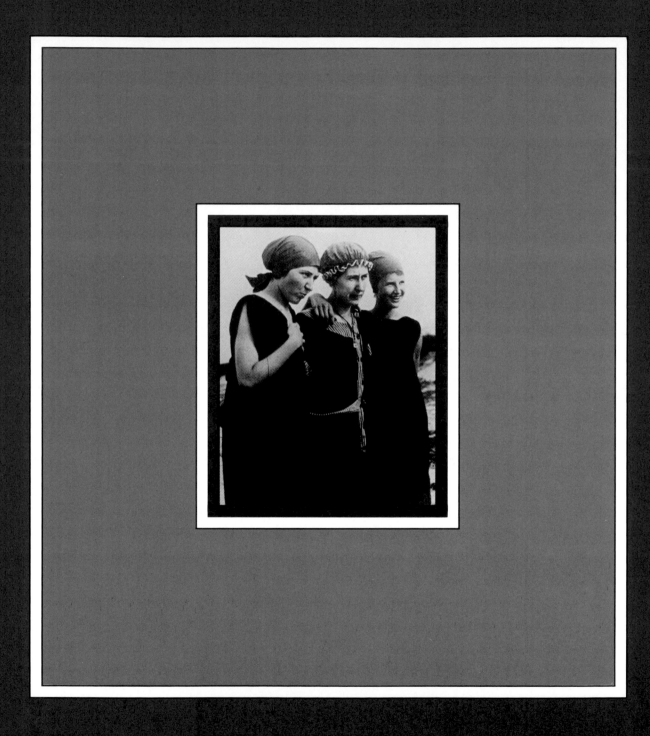

A New Century

1900~1930

Believe it or not, it was "only yesterday" that a hatless man was regarded as a curiosity and considered not completely dressed. Therefore, many stores sold nothing but men's hats. One such business was that operated by Walter J. Simmons and Company at 341 Main Street. Simmons began business in 1880 on Main Street and at one time operated another store on Granby Street after 1900. He ceased operating after 1926. Here is displayed a method of his advertising, about 1900: a large replica of a silk hat mounted on a four-wheel carriage and driven by a properly dressed coachman.

Ribbons and bows and cameos and ruffled dresses were the style when this delightful picture was taken in 1900 by an unknown photographer who just couldn't resist preserving it for posterity. Friends of the Taylor family, they are summering at a place called Clifton Springs. Courtesy of Cecelia Taylor

Early in the twentieth century wild game was served in local restaurants and also sold in the marketplace and in such stores as the grocery of A. C. Ward, located on the southeast corner of Wolfe (now Market) Street and Market Place (now Brewer Street). This picture shows the results of a good day's hunting. Ward is reputed to have owned the small grocery store and gas station on the northwest corner of Granby Street and Sewell's Point (now Little Creek Road) that gave Ward's Corner its name. Courtesy of James Jordan IV

Freemason Street from Dunmore Street looking east in 1902 and 1980.

Many of the old homes in this block have been torn down, and the townhouses on the right have re-

placed some of them. Photograph by Carroll Walker

The Columbia Building disappeared from the Norfolk scene many years ago. The six-story structure on Granby Street between Plume and Main streets was built about 1893. On the early morning of January 31, 1902, fire broke out and spread rapidly through the building, engulfing the Atlantic Hotel on the south side and the Virginia Club Building on the north, destroying the entire block. The paper reported that when the flames reached a storage room of a saloon in the building, the whiskey stored there exploded with such force that the concussion shattered windows on the other side of the street. A complete loss, the building was never rebuilt. Photograph courtesy of Kirn Memorial Library. The inset picture taken from Plume Street shows only a wall remaining of the Columbia Building

In 1872 Atlantic City was a separate village with many small industries and stores, near the site of Old Fort Norfolk. In that year Atlantic City was connected to York Street by a new bridge. In February 1890 it was annexed to Norfolk. This picture, taken in 1903, shows the bridge, which was replaced in 1963. The body of water in the foreground is the Hague, then called Smith's Creek and in earlier days Colley's Creek. In the foreground is the newly constructed Mowbray Arch. Courtesy of Mrs. Hunter Savage

On the back of a small photograph from which this picture was made was the inscription "McCullough's Dock ...taken on Jan. 1, 1904, through the iron grating," which was atop the west wall (the last vestige) of the old stone bridge that was built over Back Town Creek in 1818, joining "North" Granby Street with the newly created "South" Granby Street extending to Main Street. City Hall Avenue came into existence about 1884 after Back Town Creek had been filled in to Granby Street. This picture shows the last of the creek not fully filled in, extending from Granby Street to Boush Street. McCullough's Dock is on the right. In the center behind it a tug is placing a car float alongside the pier of the Norfolk, New York and Philadelphia (later PRR) Railroad. The C&O Railway had a warehouse-pier on the other side. A section of the Anheuser Busch Brewing Company is on the right. Within the next year or so the creek would be filled in and Boush Street extended to Main Street. Courtesy of Mrs. Hunter Savage

The intersection of Boush Street and College Place looking north as it appeared in 1904. The large tree in the center of the picture grew on the property of C. Whittle Sams, Norfolk lawyer and historian, whose house was built in 1804 by the great-great-grandson of Samuel Boush, first mayor of Norfolk Borough in 1736. When Boush Street was widened about 1929, the tree was taken down and Sams's house was moved back several feet. Courtesy of Mrs. Hunter Savage

The intersection of Boush Street and College Place in 1980. The building on the right is the Norfolk College Building, once the site of the Rochambeau Apartments built about 1904. All of the houses shown in the 1904 picture have disappeared. The Merrimac Apartments, Epworth Methodist Church, and the Chesapeake and Potomac Telephone Building are shown in the center. The Merrimac Apartments are now being demolished. Photograph by Carroll Walker

A sad day at the beach. According to the person who took this picture on June 2, 1904, the two dressed-up youngsters with the broad-brimmed hats are being punished for some reason and are not permitted to go wading with the other children. Courtesy of Mrs. Hunter Savage

It is claimed that this 1902 Rambler, owned by Walter J. Adams, the father of Norfolk physician Dr. Walter P. Adams, was the first gasoline car in Norfolk. It cranked up on the side and was steered by a lever; the engine was under the seat; and it used bicycle tires. The car carried Virginia State License Number 1—until that number was assigned to the governor in 1905 or 1906. The three children are, left to right: Berryman Green, Forstall Adams, and Walter P. Adams (later the doctor). Mr. and Mrs. Adams accompany the children. Courtesy of Dr. Walter P. Adams

This delightful picture of Smith's Creek (now the Hague) and the Second Presbyterian Church was taken in 1904 shortly after the church was built. The small bridge in the upper center left was a footbridge connecting Yarmouth Street with Fairfax Avenue. The long structure in the center is a streetcar trestle for cars that ran from Boush Street to Tazewell and Dunmore streets and over the trestle to Mowbray Arch, where the car turned right and went north. The tracks in the lower part lead to the Ghent Bridge, which cannot be seen. This picture was taken from the third floor of a house on Mowbray Arch. The 1980 inset picture by Carroll Walker shows the same area, seventy-seven years later, photographed from the same room of the house from which the 1904 picture was taken. Much of the creek has been filled in, the other two bridges have been demolished, and the old Ghent Bridge has been turned into a pedestrian walk. The church still stands, now occupied by the Unitarian Church. The white building in the center is the newspaper building. The Hague Towers, built in the early 1960s, dominates the area. Courtesy of Mrs. Hunter Savage

Over the years many changes have taken place on Granby Street, particularly the College Place area. These three pictures are typical. The first picture was taken in 1904 looking north on Granby Street from the present location of Smith and Welton department store. On the left is the Norfolk College for Young Ladies, built about 1880. With the exception of the Leache Wood Seminary on the corner of Freemason and Granby streets, which can be seen just left of the buggy, all other buildings in this block were residences. Courtesy of Mrs. Hunter Savage

The second picture shows the same area as it appeared about 1922. Although the college had ceased operations around 1900, the building still remained, the lower part being converted to stores. For a while it operated as the Algonquin Hotel and later the Lee Hotel. The Hotel Norfolk was originally the Colonial Hotel, built in 1905, and the Leache-Wood Seminary gave way to the Lynnhaven Hotel in 1907, later the Southland Hotel and now the Commodore Maury Hotel. The building in the distance is the Flatiron Building, built in 1918 to house naval operations. The arch lights were erected in 1909 and taken down about 1925. Photograph by Harry C. Mann; courtesy of Kirn Memorial Library

In an effort to make Granby Street more attractive to shoppers and to revitalize downtown, the street was converted to the Granby Mall. Streetcar tracks were pulled up and the street repaved, trees and flower containers added. The same old buildings are standing: the college building is boarded up, the lower front part given over to small shops; the Colonial-Norfolk Hotel is in disuse. The Lynnhaven-Southland Hotel has been renovated and renamed the Commodore Maury. In the distance are the old Ames and Bownley and Flatiron buildings. In this picture an art show is in progress. Photograph by Carroll Walker, 1980

One of Norfolk's early office buildings was the Law Building, located on the northwest corner of Plume and Granby streets. Built on the site of the old Cincinnatus Newton property in 1905, the building consisted of two sections as shown in this picture. In 1922 a third section on Randolph and Plume streets was added. Courtesy of J. B. Denny, Jr.

Members of the Norfolk High School football team posed for this picture in 1905. This was Norfolk's first such team. The high school, located on the corner of Louitt and Park avenues in Brambleton, is shown in the inset picture. It was owned by the Hemenway family, who had converted it into a boys' school. Acquired by the city in 1894, it became Norfolk's first high school. A fire in the building in 1908 necessitated moving the students temporarily to the newly built John Marshall School on Omohundro Avenue. By 1911 Maury High School was built, and all Norfolk High School students were transferred there. The only identifiable person in the picture is Arthur Billups, who is on the first row right with his hand on his legs. Courtesy of Mary Arthur Soudemire

In the early 1900s an interesting pastime was to watch cigars made by hand in the front windows of Norfolk's many cigar stores. This picture taken about 1906 shows one such "manufactory" and was believed to have been located on Main Street. The men sitting in their stalls with their molds before them placed an unbroken leaf in the mold, to which strips of filler tobacco were added. The tobacco was pressed tightly for shaping after which another leaf was wound around it for the finished product. Note the packages of finished cigars between the men. Courtesy of Mrs. Sandy Parsons

—From the Ledger-Dispatch, 1910.

THE LARCHMONT 'JITNEY'

When Bellamy and Hough began the development of Larchmont people said they were crazy because only a fool would want his home five miles from his office. Be that as it may, the first house was sold in 1908, and others quickly followed.

In 1909, in order to induce people to move to Larchmont, T. Marshall Bellamy inaugurated a bus service from Commercial Place, the fare for which was a nickel or, as commonly known in those days, a "jitney." The buses were soon called jitney buses, and a book of tickets could be purchased for $2.25. Jitnies would hold twenty people and the ride took about twenty minutes. Courtesy of T. Carroll Bellamy

This was the office of Bellamy and Hough, 83 Plume Street, as it appeared in 1905. They were aggressive real estate developers, perhaps best known for their development of Larchmont in 1907, an attractive area about five miles north from downtown Norfolk. John W. Hough is shown at left and T. Marshall Bellamy at right; the center person is unidentified. Courtesy of T. Carroll Bellamy

Taken about 1907, this scene shows a small chapel on the corner of Stockley Gardens and Olney Road in Ghent. Known as St. Stephens Episcopal Chapel, it appears to have been built around 1906. About 1909, Christ Episcopal Church, then located on Freemason Street, acquired the property and constructed a church on the site, opening it for services in 1911. During the 1930s this church consolidated with St. Luke's Episcopal Church and became known as Christ and St. Luke's Episcopal Church. The inset picture shows the church as it appears in 1980. Courtesy of Kirn Memorial Library

In 1907 small watercraft are tied up at the piers and warehouses of the Old Dominion Steamship Company at the foot of Church Street (now St. Paul Boulevard), loaded with baskets of fresh produce from the various farms located on the many waterways in Tidewater Virginia and Eastern North Carolina. Before the advent of highways and trucks, boats were often the only way a farmer could get his produce to the city for transshipment beyond. Courtesy of H. D. Eluto

By 1914, when this panoramic picture was taken by Harry C. Mann from the balcony of a house on the southwest corner of Manchester Avenue and Hampton Boulevard, there were hundreds of substantial homes in Larchmont, and many new ones were built. The sweep of this picture takes in Manchester Avenue on the left to the old Vanderberry farm on the center right. Hampton Boulevard is in the foreground. Courtesy of N. T. Bundy, Jr.

The Norfolk and Western Railway's coal piers at Lambert's Point in 1907. While the tonnage carried by steam vessels was continually increasing, the old sailing vessel was still in demand, as is evidenced by the masts of schooners. A six-master (right) is taking on coal at the piers. Courtesy of H.D. Eluto

View of Norfolk harbor looking west from the National Bank of Commerce in 1907. On the extreme left a portion of the Atlantic Hotel can be seen. Next to it is the Virginia Club Building and across the street the first two sections of the Law Building. The third section would be built in 1922. In front of the Law Bulding is the Chamberlain Building, beneath which is the Neddo Hotel on Plume Street. The dead end of Botetourt Street can be seen above the right of the Law Building. Atlantic City is in the center, and in the habor are two schooners, one of which (center) appears to be under sail. Courtesy of H. D. Eluto

The Virginian Railway coal piers 1 and 2 at Sewell's Point. The Virginian Railway came into Norfolk in September 1909, operating as such until merged with the Norfolk and Western Railway in 1961. The N&W continued to operate the piers until the early seventies, when the property was acquired by the U.S. Navy and made a part of the Naval Operating Base. Courtesy of Norfolk Historical Society

What the well-dressed woman wore when she went bathing at Ocean View in 1907. From head to foot she was well protected from the sun, the mosquitos, and the leering stares of wicked men. *Courtesy of Al and Vic Doumar*

Commercial Place has always been the heart of Norfolk. Looking west on Main Street, this picture shows the area about 1907. In the center can be seen the old Citizens National Bank Building, next to which was the conical-top YMCA. The tall building on the right is the new National Bank of Commerce Building, built in 1905. On the corner of Main and Bank Streets, behind the streetcar, is the Marine Bank (columned front). The car tracks terminated behind the Confederate Monument (not shown in this picture). *Courtesy of Kirn Memorial Library*

Commercial Place in 1980. Most of the old buildings have disappeared. In the center distance the Seaboard Bank Bulding and the Citizens Office Building, built in the early 1900s, still stand. The small striped building in the center is the Life Federal Savings and Loan Association. The old National Bank of Commerce Building has been completely renovated and has become the First and Merchants National Bank. The building on the right is the garage ramp for the Virginia National Bank, a part of which is shown on the left. When the Virginia National Bank was erected in 1965 on the location of the Confederate Monument, the latter was moved about 150 feet northeast of the bank building. A portion of its base can be seen in the extreme right. Photograph by Carroll Walker

The Neddo Hotel, located on East Plume Street just off Granby Street, was built around 1902. In its early days it was a very popular hotel. This picture was taken about 1907. The hotel was taken down in 1979. Courtesy of Chamber of Commerce

Harry C. Mann, a native of Petersburg, came to Norfolk in 1907. He knew nothing about photography; however, his brother, Col. James Mann, was one of the counsel for the Jamestown Exposition Photographic Corporation which secured the photographic concession at the exposition grounds, and Harry was appointed to a position with the company. He began photographing the uncompleted buildings and muddy ungraded streets at the unfinished exposition. He soon acquired a camera for himself and began to branch out into the photographic field, photographing, in particular, beach scenes, woodland vistas, and the moods of the various combinations of clouds, sea, and sandhills.

When the exposition closed that fall, Mann remained in Norfolk and opened a studio on the second floor of a building on the corner of Bank and Main streets. He traveled all over the state, photographing old homes, college buildings, and churches, but his first love was in Norfolk and the Cape Henry area. His work here brought him acclaim, not only in this country but in Europe as well, and he won awards in London and Paris. From time to time his work appeared in the National Geographic magazine.

Mann left Norfolk around 1924 when his health began to fail, and he passed away in Lynchburg in 1926. Norfolk is forever indebted to him for the thousands of pictures he took of his adopted city.

At the Jamestown Exposition in 1907, one of the most popular attractions was the Miller Brothers 101 Ranch of Fort Bliss, Oklahoma, a wild west show featuring cowboys, cowgirls, Indians, Mexicans, and buffaloes. The show offered such typical western activities as the robbery of a stagecoach, the capture and execution of a horsethief, the dancing of a quadrille on horseback, and an Indian raid on a covered wagon (rapidly avenged)—all performed in an enormous space. This photograph was taken by the Jamestown Photographic Corporation, of which Harry C. Mann was vice-president and general manager. Courtesy of Kirn Memorial Library

President Theodore Roosevelt addressed a gathering on Georgia Day. Courtesy of Norfolk Historical Society

At the Jamestown Exposition in 1907 an anchor was displayed supposedly from the C.S.S. Virginia (Merrimac). It is not known what became of it after the exposition closed; however, an item appeared in the Virginian-Pilot for April 19, 1911, that "an anchor carried by the Merrimac when the Confederates fought on her was dredged from the bight of Craney Island about four years ago" at the spot where the Merrimac was reported blown up. This anchor was a 6,000-pound piece of wrought iron with a huge stock of black walnut covered with copper, found in the Southern Branch of the Elizabeth River by a dredge deepening the channel to the Navy Yard. The wooden stock measured seventeen feet in length and was thirty-four inches thick and sixteen inches wide. The shank of the anchor was thirteen feet long and nine feet, seven inches from tip to tip of the flukes. Parts of the anchor showed some deterioration.

At the beginning of the War Between the States, the Merrimac was a full-rigged first class frigate lying out of commission at the Navy Yard. Evacuating the yard, the Union forces set fire to the ship and set her adrift. The ship drifted to the shallow water on the opposite shore, where she sank. When the Confederates decided to rebuild her as the Virginia along the lines of an ironclad, not a single anchor was found among her remains, so new anchors were secured from a supply at the Navy Yard.

The anchor dredged from Craney Island was subsequently bought by R.

Conversion of the Merrimac to the Confederate ironclad Virginia at the Gosport Navy Yard, Portsmouth, Virginia, 1861-62.

W. Hudgins & Sons, dealers in marine supplies, who planned to repair it and sell it "to the master of a windjammer." It is not known to whom Hudgins sold the anchor.

Over the years many people have displayed interest in the possibility of raising the Merrimac, or what was left of it, if anything. March 6, 1966, issue of the Virginian-Pilot, George H. Tucker, a well-known local historian and at one time a staff writer on the paper, wrote a well researched article on the salvaging of the Merrimac, an

operation that had extended over a period of almost ten years—from September 2, 1867, to June 2, 1876. In the conclusion of his article, Tucker stated that "according to the logbook of Dry Dock #1 at the Norfolk Navy Yard, formerly the Gosport Navy Yard, dated May 30, 1876, the Merrimac entered the dock May 30, 1876, to be cut up."

This should settle for once and for all the final disposition of the Merrimac.

This was Granby Street looking south in 1907. Almost all of the buildings shown were comparatively new. Until the construction of the Monticello Hotel (left) in 1899, business remained south of City Hall Avenue (which did not exist until 1885). After that it literally spurted up Granby Street. The Haddington Building, right of the hotel, considered Norfolk's first "skyscraper," was built about 1890. In the center right can be seen the Atlantic Hotel on Main Street, rebuilt after a disastrous fire in 1902. Next is the Law Building, the first two sections of which were built in 1905. The two buildings on the center right are the Max Schwan and Withers buildings. The Royster Building would occupy the northwest corner next to Schwan's in 1912. Picture taken from Brooke Avenue and Granby Street. Courtesy of Kirn Memorial Library

The same view in 1980. The new Federal Building at left replaced the Monticello Hotel (also the Dickson Building built around 1910). The Haddington Building and the Atlantic Hotel have been demolished. Under the Tazewell Street sign can be seen the Law Building. The tall twelve-story Royster Building, built in 1912, dominates the scene. The Schwan Building, almost hidden from sight, stands. The Withers Building, destroyed by fire, was replaced by the Lonsdale Building. The white building next to it, the Nusbaum Building, and the Tazewell building on the corner, now a hotel, were built around 1900. Photograph by Carroll Walker

This is a rare view of the west side of Granby Street between Brooke Avenue and Freemason Street, taken about 1908. The corner building at left is the Tazewell Building on Brooke Avenue and Granby Street, built about 1900. The building next to it was the Lenox Building, built a little later and totally destroyed by fire on January 1, 1918, when the Monticello Hotel burned. A smaller building was erected in its place which later was the home of the D. P. Paul Company. Next to it was the Alsace Hotel and the Lorraine Hotel on the opposite corner. In the distance can be seen the newly built Lynnhaven Hotel (now Commodore Maury Hotel). Courtesy of Kirn Memorial Library

In the early days of Norfolk, Granby Street was not well lighted. A new system was planned, and on the night of September 10, 1909, James H. Brownley, president of Ames, Brownley and Hornthal, a department store, pulled the switch that lit up Norfolk's new arch lights extending from Freemason Street to Main Street. The lights were later extended along Main Street to Church Street and then up Church Street to Queen Street (Brambleton Avenue). They were taken down around 1925. Photograph by Harry C. Mann; courtesy of C. S. Barrett

Toward the end of 1969 the city embarked upon a program to convert Granby Street to a pedestrian mall, which was completed in 1976. This picture, taken in 1976 from about the same location as Harry C. Mann's picture, shows the same area at night. The Roxy Theatre has disappeared. Photograph by Carroll Walker

A view of Warren Crescent looking north from Mill Street in Ghent in 1908. Courtesy of Kirn Memorial Library

One of the streetcars of the Norfolk and Portsmouth Traction Company on the west side of Granby Street between City Hall Avenue and Brooke Avenue in 1908. This company was taken over by the Virginia Railway and Power Co. in 1911. Courtesy of Al and Vic Doumar

For more than half a century the name Preston in Norfolk has been associated with the dance. Many people today, grown and with families of their own, fondly recall the days when they were pupils at the Preston School of Dancing on Botetourt Street.

In 1909 Miss Caperton Preston, a history and English teacher at St. George's private school on Boissevain Avenue between Colonial and Moran Avenues, began to offer dancing classes at the school. Successful from the start, Miss Preston, against the advice of her friends, opened her own studio on Botetourt Street, where she remained until her death in 1965

There was one thing about Miss Preston that her pupils will remember: whenever she wanted their immediate attention, she would put two fingers to her mouth and emit a whistle as sharp as any ever made by a man.

When Miss Preston passed away in 1965, Anne Gray Hackney, her assistant for many years, took over the operation of the school, retaining the name. The old school building is gone, but Mrs. Hackney still operates in another building on Botetourt Street just a block away.

This is possibly the earliest photograph of Miss Preston's dancing classes, taken about 1909 when she was teaching at St. George's School. The small picture by Carroll Walker shows Miss Preston's graduating class of 1963. Miss Preston is on the extreme left and Mrs. Hackney on the right. Courtesy of Anne Gray Hackney

Miss Preston was so well loved and respected by her students that they gave her a party on the fiftieth anniversary of the school. Many of her former students well up in their years came from all over the state to pay homage to her. R. K. T. "Kit" Larsen, then managing editor of the Virginian-Pilot, observed that "just think—all of these people are here this evening, some 250 miles from home, just to shake hands with a grand little lady, eat a cookie, and drink a glass of fruit punch!"

The late Grover Outland, a former state legislator attending the party (right) was asked, "When did you ever take lessons from Miss Preston?" He replied that when he lived in Southampton County in 1912, he and a friend, receiving an invitation to a dance and not knowing how to waltz, caught a train to Norfolk, went to Miss Preston's, practiced waltzing for several hours, returned to Courtland, and enjoyed the dance that night. That, he said, made him a bona fide alumnus of Miss Preston's.

Miss Preston greets guests at the fiftieth anniversary party given by students and alumni of the Preston School of Dancing in 1959 at the Hague Club. In the picture are, left to right: Mrs. Grover C. Outland, Sr., Mr. and Mrs. Webster M. Chandler (son-in-law and daughter, Nancy Outland), Miss Preston, and Mr. Outland. Photograph by Carroll Walker

In 1909 the Norfolk City Guard posed for this picture before the gaily decorated courthouse. During the period Virginia was under military occupation after the War Between the States, militia companies were not permitted to organize in the state. As soon as the occupation ended in 1871, companies began to form, the first in Norfolk being the Norfolk City Guard, organized April 9, 1871. The Norfolk Light Artillery Blues, Norfolk's oldest militia company, reorganized a few days later. In 1882, when the 4th Virginia Regiment, Virginia Volunteers, was formed, the Norfolk City Guard was assigned to it as Company B. When the National Guard was organized in 1905, the Norfolk City Guard became a part of that organization. Upon the entry of the United States in World War I in April 1917, the 4th Virginia Regiment was called into active service and sent to Alabama for training, with most of the men absorbed into the 116th Infantry, which sailed shortly for France. The company never reorganized. Courtesy of Mrs. Charles H. McCoy

On November 19, 1909, President William H. Taft visited Norfolk to attend the second annual convention of the Atlantic Deeper Waterways Commission at the Monticello Hotel. This picture shows President Taft in a parade as it turned the corner at Granby and Main streets. After the meeting was over, the presidential party ended the visit by attending a sumptuous banquet at O'Keeffe's famous restaurant at Cape Henry where he feasted to his heart's content on oysters, in particular. Courtesy of Mrs. Dorothy Johnson

The dedication ceremony in 1909 on the opening of the new Navy YMCA located on the corner of Boush Street and Brooke Avenue. Made possible by John D. Rockefeller, over the years it served the Navy well, but with changing times it gradually fell into disuse. It is now used by the Union Mission. Its future at this time is questionable. Note the streetcar on Boush Street and the ice wagon next to it. Courtesy of Kirn Memorial Library. 1980 Photograph by Caroll Walker

The extreme end of Botetourt Street below Freemason Street was a quiet, pleasant area with an unobstructed view of the river. The houses shown here were built sometime in the 1870s; the picture was taken about 1910. A section of the Monticello Hotel, built in 1898, can be seen on the right. The building a little behind the first house is the Navy "Y" on Boush Street, built in 1909. Courtesy of Alice Jaffe

A late 1980 view of lower Botetourt Street. Once a dead-end street, it now meets with College Place, which in turn has been extended to Botetourt Street. The old houses in the other picture were demolished years ago. In their place new townhouses have been built on the street and on College Place as well. The area, once known as Smith's Point, is now called Freemason Harbour. The old seawall (in shadow) has been rebuilt. Photograph by Carroll Walker

For many years in the early 1900s, Charles and Louis Mansbach, operators of The Hub Clothing Store on East Main Street near Church Street, gave a Christmas dinner—usually the day after Christmas to an estimated 2,000 underprivileged children of Norfolk and Portsmouth. This early flash picture taken by Harry C. Mann covers the Eighth Annual Hub Christmas Dinner held in the auditorium of the old City Market building (also known as the Armory) on City Hall Avenue on December 27, 1910. The Virginian-Pilot for that date stated that "30 tables, each thirty feet long" were piled high with food of all kinds. Gifts were also available. Courtesy of Kirn Memorial Library

This picture shows the first bridge over Tanner's Creek (now Lafayette River), built about 1903 by the Norfolk and Atlantic Electric Railway Company in the construction of a streetcar line from downtown Norfolk to Pine Beach, which was located at the west end of Taussig Boulevard where the Newport News-Norfolk ferry once docked. The 1910 photograph was taken from the drawspan in the center of the bridge, looking south toward the then-new suburb of Larchmont. Courtesy of William L. Tazewell

This circa-1915 view looks north from the site of the U.S. Public Service Hospital, built in 1917. Courtesy of Kirn Memorial Library

The Italian Baroque Room in the Chrysler Museum. Courtesy of The Chrysler Museum

One of the Chrysler Museum's treasures: Paul Gaugin's oil on canvas, La Perte du Pucelage, 1890. Courtesy of The Chrysler Museum, Norfolk, Virginia

In 1905 alumnae of the Leache-Wood Seminary for young ladies, located on the present site of the Commodore Maury Hotel on the corner of Freemason and Granby streets, conceived the idea of a museum for Norfolk. Their early meetings were held in the public library on Freemason Street, where their collection was stored. In 1914 the Irene Leache Art Association was founded for the purpose of securing better housing and care of the collection.

When the group became known as the Norfolk Society of Arts around 1917 and continued their drive for a museum, the city gave them a site in the Lee Park area, facing the Hague, which area shortly before had been a part of Smith's Creek extending at one time almost to Church Street. In this pre-1910 view of Lee Park the three bridges are the Ghent Bridge, a streetcar trestle, and a footbridge connecting Yarmouth Street with Fairfax Avenue.

The society kept its small collection in the old library and then in a temporary building on the corner of Mowbray Arch and Fairfax Avenue, made possible by Florence K. Sloane. Eventually, the city agreed to appropriate $12,500 a year for maintenance and operation of the museum. Mrs. Sloane chaired a committee to raise money for construction of the museum. Despite the Depression, in 1933 the first of three units of the museum was finished. In 1939 a second unit was opened. As activities increased, membership grew, and collections were added, a new wing, known as the Willis Houston Wing, was added and opened in 1968.

In May 1971 the Norfolk Museum of Arts and Sciences merged with the Chrysler Museum of Provincetown, Massachusetts, to become the Chrysler Museum at Norfolk. Walter Chrysler has moved to Norfolk a priceless collection that has become world renowned and to which additions are continually being made. The permanent collection includes objects from ancient Greece, Rome, the Orient, and pre-Columbian America as well as European and American art. Its glass collection of 7,500 pieces is one of the largest in the United States. Photograph by Carroll Walker

Acme Photo Company photographed the new concrete bridge in 1934, looking north from atop one of the hospital buildings.

In the late 1960s the old concrete bridge was replaced by a wider and more modern bridge to accommodate the increasing flow of traffic. Photograph by Carroll Walker

Over the piers and barges of the Southern Railway at Pinners Point, laden with bales of cotton for shipment to various destinations, we get a view of Norfolk's busy harbor and skyline in 1910. The tall building in the center left is the National Bank of Commerce, then Norfolk's tallest building. The various piers along the waterfront are those of the Pennsylvania Railroad, Chesapeake and Ohio, Old Bay Line, and others. Photograph by Harry C. Mann; courtesy of Kirn Memorial Library

Commercial Place looking west in 1910 by Harry C. Mann from the W. G. Swartz Building on Main Street. A few automobiles have made their appearance, but most of the delivery work was done by "drays" lined up in the center of the street, waiting for a call. The ferries operated between Norfolk, Berkley, and Portsmouth.

The inset picture shows the Omni International Hotel built and open for business in 1975. The hotel occupies almost all of the waterfront area from Nebraska Street (by the Berkley Bridge-Tunnel) to Commerce Street. The Omni Hotel is now located on the site of the ferry docks. Photograph by Carroll Walker

Somewhere along the Norfolk waterfront around 1910 men load heavy rope on a sailing vessel. Courtesy of Norfolk Historical Society

Before the days of trucks and highways, old Roanoke Dock and the adjacent area were the center points for the unloading of products from farms located along the many waterways in eastern Virginia and North Carolina. This scene was taken in 1910—when a good watermelon could be bought for ten cents. Courtesy of Norfolk Historical Society

An interesting scene that has forever disappeared from Norfolk's waterways was that of tugs towing barges laden with logs destined to the many lumber mills in and around Norfolk for processing. Most of this traffic originated in southeastern Virginia and northeastern North Carolina. Photograph by Harry C. Mann, 1912; courtesy of N. H. Bundy, Jr.

This odd-looking gasoline-powered car, often referred to as The Scooter, was operated by the Norfolk Southern Railroad from Norfolk to Munden Point, Virginia. It began operations around 1910 and became electrified in 1923. In 1929 the Norfolk Southern withdrew it from active service, and it was broken up for scrap in 1935. Courtesy of Kirn Memorial Library

At the foot of East Main Street were the Union Station, built in 1912 and demolished in 1963, and the Norfolk Yard of the Norfolk and Western Railway. Most of the tracks shown in this picture have been taken up, and a part of Waterfront Drive, connecting with the Virginia Beach Expressway, curves through the center of the picture. Tidewater Drive is shown in the center running north. In 1680 almost all of the bottom half of this view was under water—known as Newton's Creek and later, after 1865, as Mahone's Lake. Photograph by S. H. Ringo

Prior to 1919 the passenger terminal of the Norfolk Southern's Electric Division was on City Hall Avenue at the Monticello Arcade, as shown in this picture. They had trackage rights up Monticello Avenue over the Norfolk and Atlantic Terminal Company to Eleventh Street. The latter line ran to Pine Beach, located at the western part of the Naval Base. During 1919 the Norfolk Southern discontinued the use of City Hall Avenue as a terminal and moved into the Union Station at the foot of East Main Street. This 1912 photograph shows some of their cars on City Hall Avenue. Courtesy of Kirn Memorial Library

This is the Berkley terminus of the Norfolk Southern Railroad in 1912, and the inset shows the waterside as it appeared from Portsmouth in 1897. The Norfolk Southern originally began as the Elizabeth City and Norfolk Railroad, constructed in 1881 from Berkley (Norfolk) to Elizabeth City, North Carolina, and shortly thereafter to Edenton, North Carolina. Over the years it was gradually extended to reach Charlotte, North Carolina. The railroad served a rich agricultural section, hauling cotton, lumber, naval stores, peanuts, and vegetables to its terminus in Berkley for transshipment to northern and western markets. In the 1970s the Norfolk Southern was merged with the Southern Railway, its name disappearing forever from the list of active railroads.

Norshipco (formerly the Norfolk Shipbuilding and Dry Dock Corporation) now occupies the site. Larger photograph by Harry C. Mann

In May 1910 the city began extensive street repair, beginning with Granby Street at Queen Street (Brambleton Avenue) and continuing to Main and then to and including Church Street. The expansion was to take almost two years. The old stone blocks were replaced with wooden, or as they were known, Belgian blocks. This picture shows work in the upper 300 block of Granby Street between Freemason Street and College Place. The area beyond Freemason Street was mostly residential. Courtesy of William L. Tazewell

In November 1910 the Navy's hope to launch an airplane from the deck of a ship came to fruition when on a showery November 14 Lt. Eugene B. Eley, U.S.N., took off from a wooden deck on the bow of the U.S.S. Birmingham. Through a miscalculation his plane went lower than anticipated, striking the water with a splash. However, the plane righted itself and started up. Eley made a successful run of several miles, not to Fort Monroe as originally planned but in the direction of Cape Henry, and returned—landing at Willoughby Spit. Eley contended that it would be just as easy for a plane to land on a ship whether the latter was still or in motion. The destroyer Roe is in the background serving as a plane guard. Courtesy of U.S. Naval Historical Center

Fire Station Number 6 was built in 1911 on the corner of Twelfth Street (Princess Anne Road) and Monticello Avenue. One of the vehicles was a combination hose and chemical wagon. The seventy-foot tower was used for drying hoses and for fire drills. Courtesy of Norfolk Historical Society

In 1980 the Watt, Rettew and Clay building is vacant, a Trailways Bus Line occupies the former site of the Lowenberg Building, and the striped building is the First and Merchants Bank Building (formerly the National Bank of Commerce Building). The Citizens Bank Building is now the Citizens Office Building and the Y.M.C.A. has disappeared. The new Virginia National Bank on old Commercial Place now dominates the area. Photograph by Carroll Walker

Looking east on Main Street from Granby Street as it appeared in 1911. The Watt, Rettew and Clay Building and the Lowenberg Building are on the left. On the right are the Customs House, the Citizens National Bank Building, and the YMCA. Courtesy of Kirn Memorial Library

This picture appeared in the Virginian-Pilot on December 24, 1911, announcing that the buildings on the northwest corner of City Hall Avenue and Granby Street would be torn down and a new twelve-story office building known as the Royster Building would be erected the following year. For a year or so a moving picture theatre known as the Gaiety Theatre occupied the space next to Max Schwan's. This theatre had no relationship to the Gaiety burlesque theatre on East Main Street in later years. Courtesy of Kirn Memorial Library

Where once were water and marshland, pilings are being driven as a foundation for the construction of the now twelve-story Royster Building on the northwest corner of City Hall and Granby streets. The building was begun about January 1, 1912, and was finished by the end of the year, renting office space shortly after January 1, 1913. It was stated that more than 1,700 piles were driven for the foundation. Photograph by Harry C. Mann; courtesy of Virginia State Library

This panoramic picture of Norfolk's waterfront was taken by Harry C. Mann in 1913 from Berkley and shows the area from Towne Point on the left to the Union Station at the end of East Main Street on the far right. Barges, ferries, and other watercraft move about the river. An Old Bay Line steamer is docked at its pier at Towne Point while just below it is the little paddle-wheel steamer Luray of the Old Dominion Line, which operated between Norfolk and points on the Nansemond and James Rivers. Norfolk's two "skyscrapers," the Royster Building (white) and the National Bank of Commerce Building, jut above the skyline. Three ferries are in operation, the small one in the foreground headed for its dock at the foot of Pear Street in Berkley. The Old Dominion Steamship Company's docks, showing two vessels berthed, are left of center. In addition to its river sailings, the line had a regular daily service between Norfolk and New York. The Union Station on the extreme right opened in 1913. Courtesy of N. H. Bundy, Jr.

Harry C. Mann took this panoramic picture from the National Bank of Commerce Building (now First and Merchants National Bank) about 1913. In the center left is the rebuilt Atlantic Hotel and the Virginia Club building, both destroyed in a disastrous fire in 1902. Across the street are the first two sections of the Law Building, built in 1905. A third section would be added in 1922. The new white Royster Building began operating in 1913. Across the street is the six-story Monticello Hotel, built in 1898, totally destroyed by fire in 1918, and rebuilt early in 1919. The turreted center building is the old City Market and Armory, built about 1892. It extended from City Hall Avenue to Market Street. The church steeple in the center is that of the Freemason Street Baptist Church on the corner of Freemason and Bank streets. Slightly to its left is the tower of the First Baptist Church on East Bute Street. The old Courthouse, built in 1850, is just above the old Southern Bell Telephone Company building on Plume Street. In the center right can be seen the steeples of the First Presbyterian Church on Church Street, the congregation of which had moved to a new building on Redgate and Colonial Avenue, and St. Mary's Catholic Church on Holt Street. Courtesy of N. H. Bundy, Jr.

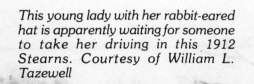

This young lady with her rabbit-eared hat is apparently waiting for someone to take her driving in this 1912 Stearns. Courtesy of William L. Tazewell

In 1912 these gay young blades stop by for a chat in a 1912 Stearns somewhere on Pembroke or Fairfax Avenue. Courtesy of William L. Tazewell

This 1912 mud-splattered Packard finds itself stuck somewhere on the old Norfolk-Suffolk Road. Courtesy of William L. Tazewell

A picture of the W. W. Lamb house on West Bute Street appears in the first Norfolk: A Pictorial History, *but it is shown here as it appeared in 1912, together with two interior views not available at that time. The house was built in 1845 and was originally named Kenmur after the family estate in Scotland. Lamb was mayor of Norfolk when the city surrendered to federal forces in 1862, and he was imprisoned at Fort Monroe.*

Legend maintains that Norfolk's historic Mace was hidden by Lamb under one of the hearths in the house during the war and forgotten for years until found in 1884.

The two interiors, taken about 1890, show the living room and library. Frederick Herman, a local architect, has acquired the house and uses it as an office and residence. Courtesy of Frederick Herman

In 1912 that part of East Main Street extending east from Bank Street, as shown in this picture, was a busy place. The Marine Bank was on the southwest corner and the popular department store of Miller, Rhoads and Swartz faced Commercial Place. Postcard from the Barton Myers Collection

This 1980 picture shows how East Main Street has changed. All the buildings in the 1912 picture have disappeared. The garage ramp of the Virginia National Bank is on the left, its entrance being across the street. Behind the ramp is the United Virginia Bank and just below it the Plaza One Building on the corner of St. Paul Boulevard and The Mall, as this part of East Main Street is now called. The flat building in the center is the new city jail. First Virginia Bank is on the right. The Confederate Monument was moved about 150 feet northeast of its former position on Commercial Place when the Virginia National Bank was built. Photograph by Carroll Walker, 1980

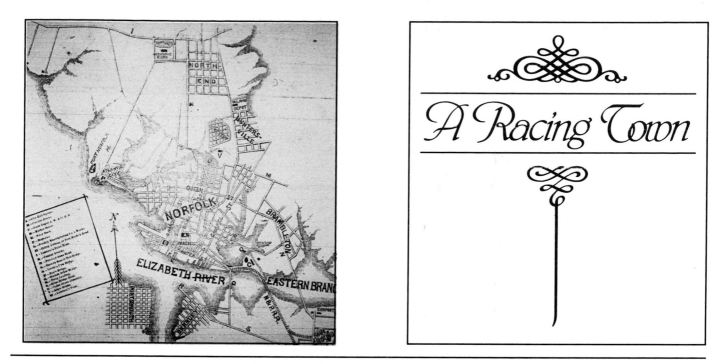

Racing has always been popular and horse racing the king of all races. In colonial days, horse racing of any kind was an active sport, and many plantations had tracks of various sizes. A country fair was also a good excuse for horse racing. After the Revolution the sport continued—and increased. In 1802 a four-day racing event was held at the Thoroughgood farm in old Princess Anne County.

In the early part of the nineteenth century many "jockey clubs" sprang up in Virginia, particularly in the Richmond-Warrenton area. Closer to Norfolk there were such clubs in Gloucester County, Southampton County, and Portsmouth.

In the April 15, 1826, issue of the American Beacon, announcement was made of the formation of the Norfolk Jockey Club, which held its first races on May 26, 1826, for two days. Another set of two races was held in October of that year. The following year, 1827, and thereafter, races of four days each were held regularly in the spring and fall—apparently well into the late 1840s. Races were held also at a track known as "Christian's Course" and later "Garrison's Course." While the precise locations of these tracks is not clear, they were probably not too far from the city. In the 1820s Norfolk barely extended beyond York Street; therefore some people speculate that the track may have been in the Lambert's Point area. There is some justification for this idea.

Burton's History of Norfolk, for example, refers to a "Julapi Hospital at Lambert's Point" where yellow fever victims were sent in 1855. In the Richmond Dispatch for September 3, 1855, reference is also made to a "Juleppi Hospital situated on the Elizabeth River, two miles from the city, and in full view of Craney Island, the James River and Hampton Roads," which was selected by the board of health as a place for yellow fever victims. The Dispatch further states that the site was "formerly a race track course, the semi-annual resort of lovers of the turf" having a "wide and level track." The clubhouse is described as "a long building, some hundred and more feet, by thirty wide, and of two stories height...situated about two hundred yards from the river's bank." Stables on the property were fitted up for the sick, and a small dwelling close by was used by nurses and physicians. Apparently, races were held here for many years. Although the exact location of this track is also unknown, persistent reports place it in the general vicinity of present-day Powhatan Avenue on Forty-Second Street in Lambert's Point near Bowden's Ferry Road, which was farmland at that time.

In 1872 at the intersection of what is now Colley Avenue (then Fort Norfolk Road) and the Lambert's Point Road (between Thirty-Third and Thirty-Fourth streets), a half-mile trotting track was located in what was then called Roanoke Park. The track seems to have been operated by the Norfolk Turf Association, but it is not known how long it was in existence.

In the October 20, 1872, issue of the Norfolk Journal the opening was announced of a "new Fair Grounds" of thirty acres, located on the property of Frederick Wilson in the Campostella section of Berkley. A half-mile track was located on the grounds. Today this would be, generally speaking, between Wilson Road and Campostella Road, not far from the Giant Open Air market. The Atlantic, Mississippi and Ohio Railroad (later the Norfolk and Western Railroad) ran special trains from its station in Norfolk to the fair grounds. The fair grounds are at lower right on this map.

Sometime before 1900 a race track and fair grounds had been established in the general area of Tidewater Drive (Old Cottage Toll Road), Chesapeake and Lafayette Boulevards, and Cromwell Road. It was apparently operated by a John Mariner and had several names: Mariner's Park, Mariner's Race Track, Lafayette Race Track, and Fair Grounds Race Track. Over the years it was used by trotters, harness racers, some horse racers, motorcycles, and automobiles. This half-mile track operated until sometime in the 1950s.

In this 1912 picture three cars get ready to race at the fair grounds. The inset shows the grandstand in 1921. Although not an airfield, the fair grounds sometimes featured small plane flying exhibitions. *Courtesy of William L. Tazewell*

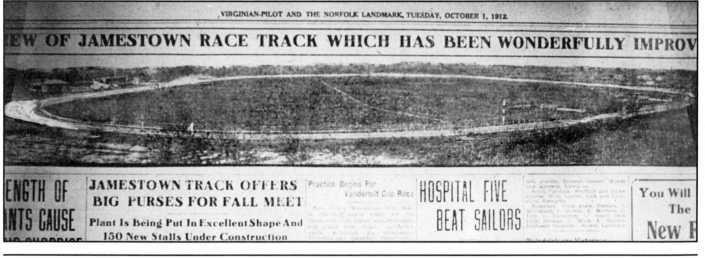

VIRGINIAN-PILOT AND THE NORFOLK LANDMARK, TUESDAY, OCTOBER 1, 1912.

EW OF JAMESTOWN RACE TRACK WHICH HAS BEEN WONDERFULLY IMPROV

ENGTH OF
NTS CAUSE

JAMESTOWN TRACK OFFERS
BIG PURSES FOR FALL MEET
Plant Is Being Put In Excellent Shape And
150 New Stalls Under Construction

Practice Begins For
Vanderbilt Cup Race

HOSPITAL FIVE
BEAT SAILORS

You Will
The
New F

Other tracks have come and gone over the years. In the early 1900s a small track was located on the Vanderberry farm in Larchmont. There is no vestige of it today and only a few people vaguely recall it. Another half-mile track was located around 1920 on the old Widgeon Farm just west of the intersection of Granby Street and Bay View Boulevard. Horses, motorcycles, and automobiles used it, but it lasted only a few years. A small race track known as Smith's was in the northwest section of Ballentine Boulevard and Virginia Beach Boulevard. This half-mile track for horses was operated by blacks.

In the early 1930s the Princess Anne Speedway began operating in the general area roughly bounded by Kempsville Road, Virginia Beach Boulevard, and Military Highway in the vicinity of the Lake Taylor Hospital. This half-mile track was used mostly by automobiles; a smaller quarter-mile track known as the Aquacade operated close by. Another track known as the Virginia Beach Speedway operated at the intersection of Witch Duck Road and Virginia Beach Boulevard. Automobile racing was popular here on a half-mile track. It ceased to operate in the 1950s.

But the biggest and best-known track of them all was the mile-long track of the Jamestown Jockey Association, located off Hampton Boulevard (then Atlantic Boulevard) where the tanks of the Exxon Corporation are today. It operated for four years, from April 1910 to April 1914, when Governor Henry C. Stuart closed it down.

At the Jamestown Jockey Association races were held twice a year, in April and around November (state laws did not permit horse racing from December 1 to March 31). Such prominent people as Thomas Fortune Ryan, traction magnate; August Belmont, president of the New York Jockey Club; and Harry Payne Whitney gave it their enthusiastic support, racing their best horses there. It had the approval of the New York Jockey Club.

Norfolk was well-liked by the racing crowd and praised by sports writers. In 1910 the New York Telegraph sent O'Neil Sevier, "the highest priced and most talented turf writer in the country," to Norfolk. He reported to his New York office Norfolk's "glowing ways." In one account he stated that "while Norfolk was not as big a town in comparison with New York, the people were hearty and hospitable, the hotels fine and their charges reasonable, and the climate excellent."

Sevier further observed that "they have real Smithfield ham here, and it

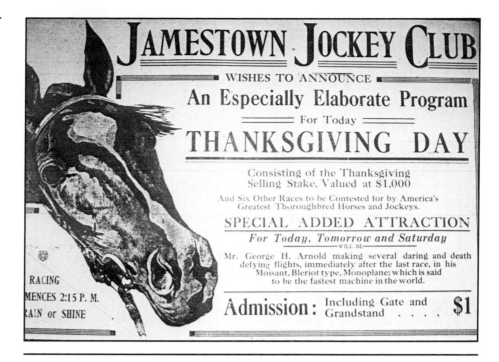

goes well with fresh, old-fashioned hen fruit...and the effect is positively poetic when one has one's ham and eggs in the dining room of the Monticello Hotel five stories up and looks out upon the Elizabeth River..."

River..."

This advertisement appeared in the Virginian-Pilot to announce the Thanksgiving program in 1912.

After the racing had ended in the fall of 1910, reports began to reach Governor William H. Mann in Richmond that bookmakers were taking bets at the Jamestown track, contrary to state law. Although officials denied the reports, the stories persisted, and in April 1911, at the start of the new season, a number of bookies were arrested. The case, however, ended in mistrial.

Many people felt that Governor Mann was unfair in his efforts to revoke the charter of the jockey club. An editorial in the Virginian-Pilot for April 17, 1911, pointed out that gambling was observed at the "Richmond State Fair last fall" and that "there was bookmaking on the races under the grandstand with the usual show of gambling paraphernalia used by the bookies much in evidence" which was supplemented with a "bar with tons of whiskey ladled out to a thirsty crowd" and that no criticism had come from the Richmond News-Leader or any other paper. When the state attorney general was asked about this, he replied that "Richmond was another matter."

Nonetheless, Governor Mann was determined to close the Norfolk track,

HARRY PAYNE WHITNEY HIS HORSE "CHEROKEE"

and when he was succeeded in 1914 by Governor Henry C. Stuart, the latter continued Mann's drive to stamp out gambling at the Jamestown track—which meant to close it down.

Despite the controversy, Norfolk's reputation grew. While the races were on, the city thronged with visitors and the hotels were packed. One man reminisced that the lobby of the Monticello Hotel looked like New Year's Eve in New York City during the racing season. But the races also attracted gambling and prostitution.

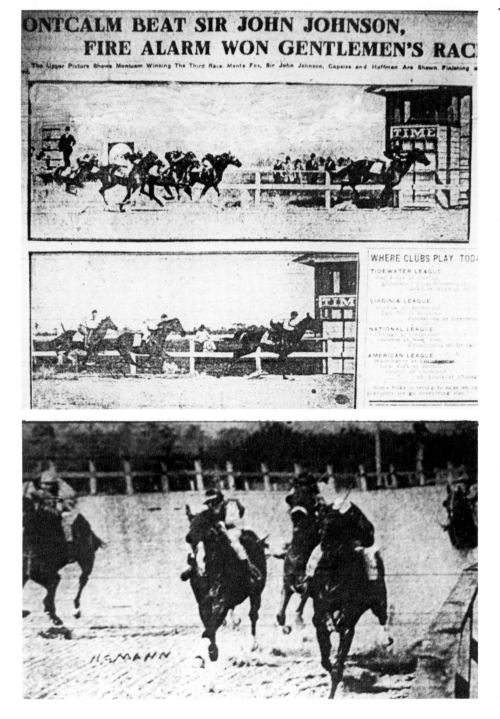

ONTCALM BEAT SIR JOHN JOHNSON,
FIRE ALARM WON GENTLEMEN'S RAC

The Upper Picture Shows Montcam Winning The Third Race. Monts Fox, Sir John Johnson, Capsize and Hoffman Are Shown Finishing

WHERE CLUBS PLAY TODA

When the April 1914 season opened Governor Stuart sent Attorney General John Garland Pollard to Norfolk. Pollard made his headquarters at the Monticello Hotel and appointed attorney S. Burnell Bragg as a special prosecutor to handle the cases of those arrested. Bragg received so many threats against himself and his family that he sent his wife and children to Petersburg. While they were gone, two attempts were made to burn their house; the second was successful, and on April 6, 1913, their house was burned.

On April 6 Governor Stuart stated that he would close the track "if it was necessary to send troops." However, instead of troops, on the late afternoon of April 7, in a surprise move, the governor sent twenty deputized Baldwin detectives, brandishing revolvers and rifles, to arrest what bookies they could find.

Several men, now in their eighties, recall well the afternoon of the raid. They agreed that at first it appeared to be a joke, someone making a "wild west movie." But as the seriousness became evident, they left. Fourteen people were arrested and charged with bookmaking.

When the leader of the raid requested that the motorman of a streetcar at the races take the men to Ocean View for jailing, the motorman refused. The detective threatened to confiscate the car and operate it himself. At this the motorman jumped off the car with the control in his hand. When the detectives tried to commandeer some automobiles, the cars "conveniently" broke down. Later on, they finally got the prisoners to the Portsmouth jail.

An attempt to race the following day failed—and the horse races ended April 10, 1914. A few automobile races were held in May, but they couldn't compare with the excitement of the horses.

Anyway, it was fun while it lasted.

Not long after automobiles appeared, people wanted to test their racing ability. As early as 1912 automobile races were held at the Norfolk Fair Grounds adjacent to present-day Fairmount Park. After the Jamestown Jockey Club closed in April 1914, some automobile racing took place there.

This four-cylinder Duesenberg is shown at the old Fair Grounds track in 1924.

Gottleib Daimler, a German engineer, is generally credited as having invented the first motorcycle by attaching a four-stroke piston to a wooden bicycle frame in 1885. It remained mostly experimental for the next few years, and not until after 1900, with continued improvements, did it develop into a dependable vehicle. Then sales began to increase. This picture of the Twin City Motorcycle Club, believed to be the first of its kind in Norfolk, was taken in 1913 by Harry C. Mann in front of the Confederate Monument on old Commercial Place. Its president was a Mack Gregory who sold motorcycles at 118 City Hall Avenue. Courtesy of N. H. Bundy, Jr.

After the turn of the century, racing motorcycles became a popular sport. These cyclists are coming in at the finish at the old Fair Grounds in 1912. Courtesy of William L. Tazewell

In 1912 Norfolk's new Y.M.C.A. was opened on the corner of Freemason and Granby streets on the site of the old Merrimack Club. It had formerly been located on East Main Street next to the Citizens Bank Building. The building contained two and one half floors of sleeping rooms, a night schoolroom, reading, game and lunch rooms, kitchen, running track, assembly hall, gym, basement bowling alley, locker rooms, baths, and a large swimming pool. The building was acquired by Rices department store in the early thirties, and the Y moved its activities to West Bute Street. Later, Rices moved across the street to its present building, and the Y building was acquired by F. W. Woolworth and Company, which is still there. It is of interest to note that the swimming pool is still in the basement—but now used for storage instead of swimming. The inset shows the lobby. Photograph by Harry C. Mann

This panoramic view of Ghent was taken from atop the Botetourt Apartments by Harry C. Mann in 1912 and shows how much the area had grown since it was first laid out in 1890. The name "Ghent" was taken from Ghent, Belgium, where the Treaty of Ghent was signed on February 17, 1815, ending the War of 1812 between the United States and Great Britain. James Moran, who owned this tract of land which was originally called Pleasant Point, changed the name to Ghent when he heard of the signing of the peace treaty. In 1830 Richard Drummond bought Ghent and lived there until his death. When the Ghent section was laid out in 1890, the old name was retained.

This new neighborhood developed rapidly, and within ten years it was filled with lovely homes, many of which are still standing. The old wooden Drummond Bridge connecting Botetourt Street with the farm was taken down about 1894 and replaced with a new structure. This bridge, in turn, was replaced about 1970 with a new pedestrian walkway.

Christ Church (now Christ and St. Luke's Episcopal Church) is visible in the upper left, and Maury High School is seen in the upper right. A car moves across the streetcar trestle on the right, which ran up Boush Street to Tazewell Street, thence to Dunmore Street, crossing the trestle and turning right on Mowbray Arch. The Drummond home was located on the site of the Holland Apartments at the foot of the bridge. Courtesy of Kirn Memorial Library

East Main Street from the old Academy of Music Building (now Selden Arcade) looking east towards Church Street as it appeared in 1912. The tall building on the left is the old National Bank of Commerce Building.

Looking east on East Main in 1980. The Selden Arcade on the left is on the site of the Academy of Music Building and a portion of the First and Merchants National Bank on Atlantic and Main streets can be seen on the left. The striped building in the center is the new First Virginia Bank Building on the corner of The Mall and St. Paul Boulevard. The building in the upper right is the Virginia National Bank Building. Photograph by Carroll Walker.

For years the Sansone Fruit Company was located on East Main Street at the head of Commercial Place. Sansone was advertising grapes for 10¢ and 15¢ a box and Bartlett pears 25¢ a box, with each box containing at least six pears. Bananas in those days could be purchased for as little as 75¢ a bunch. Photograph by Harry C. Mann, 1912

Looking north on Granby Street from Main Street in 1913. The Atlantic Hotel was on the left as were the Virginia Club Building, Law Building, Royster Building, and others. On the corner right was the well-known ladies' ready-to-wear store of Watt, Rettew, and Clay, better known as Watt's. The store went out of business at the beginning of the Depression. Photograph by Harry C. Mann; courtesy of Kirn Memorial Library

In 1913 Schreier and Son, ladies' millinery, was located in the newly built Spratley Building on the northeast corner of Granby and Tazewell streets. This window displays some of the latest styles that the well "under" dressed woman wore in 1913. Schreier's went out of business a few years later. Shulman and Company now occupy this location. Photograph by Harry C. Mann

Judging from the sides of beef hanging outside this butcher shop in the good old summertime, refrigeration was not a must in 1913. Nor was there any extra charge for flies. This shop, located on the corner of Monticello Avenue and Wolfe (now Market) Street, was known as The Mart, operated by E. M. Bell. The woman in the wide-brim straw hat, primly dressed in white, has evidently bought a couple of fresh chickens, which she holds by their legs. Dressed chickens in plastic trays were still a long way over the horizon. Courtesy of Virginia State Library

This scene is typical of small "mom and pop" grocery stores that were prevalent at the turn of the century and for many years after. This store was located on the corner of Duke and York streets in the period between 1910 and 1913 and was operated by Shekary John. Refrigeration was not yet commonplace, judging from the wild game (ducks and rabbits) and hog carcasses on display. Two crates of chickens on each side of the store indicate that chickens were sold "live," the customer having to prepare the bird from start to finish.

The young lady on the left, possibly Mr. John's daughter, holds one or two live chickens on her lap, while the woman at right, presumably Mrs. John, fills a peck measure with greens of some kind. Fruits and vegetables in those days were invariably sold by "dry" measure, such as pints, quarts, and pecks. Weighing by the pound was not done for many years. Mr. John appears to be dressing the carcass of a hog, and leaning against the barrel beneath the hog can be seen a meat saw commonly used in "dressing" carcasses. Courtesy of Al and Vic Doumar

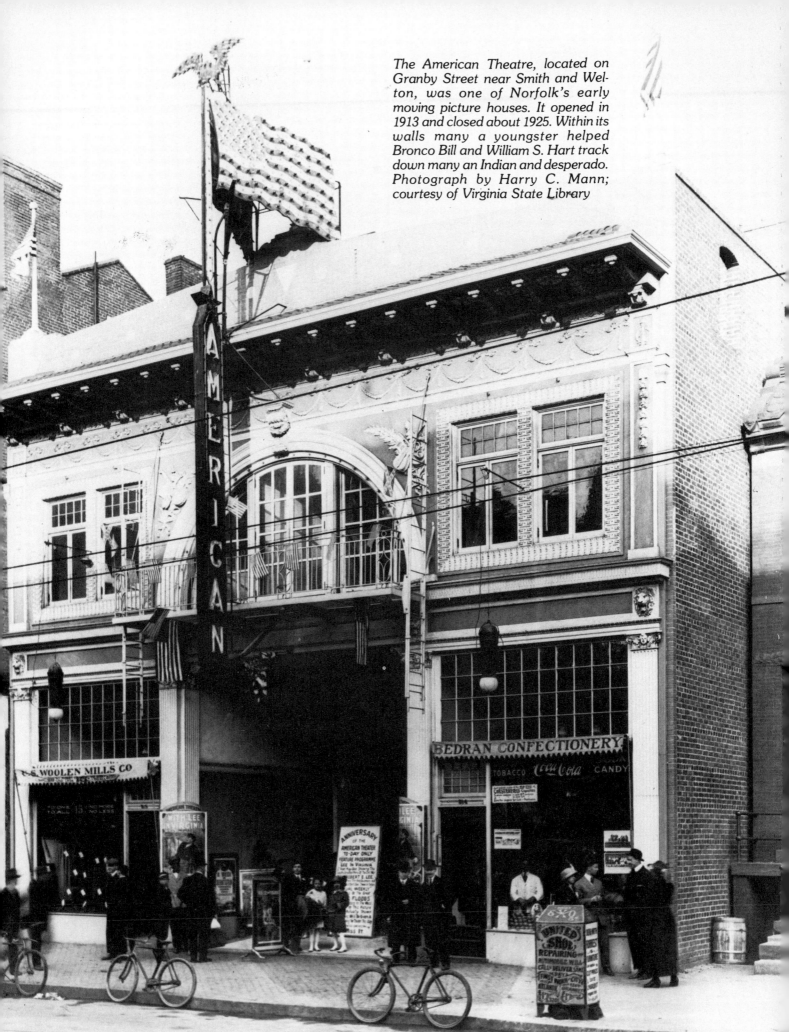

The American Theatre, located on Granby Street near Smith and Welton, was one of Norfolk's early moving picture houses. It opened in 1913 and closed about 1925. Within its walls many a youngster helped Bronco Bill and William S. Hart track down many an Indian and desperado. Photograph by Harry C. Mann; courtesy of Virginia State Library

The interior of the old National Bank of Commerce located on the corner of Main and Atlantic streets in 1913. Tellers were well protected in those days by the marble fronts and bronze cages, making the occupants less accessible to the more ambitious Jesse Jameses. Unlike the "country club" appearance of banks today, this style of interior decor was typical of banks at the early part of the century. Photograph by Harry C. Mann; courtesy of Kirn Memorial Library

Harry C. Mann took this picture in 1913 of Norfolk's first motorcycle patrol with their early Indian motorcycles. Note that only the two end machines have the old carbon lamp for illumination. All have rubber bull horns. Whether he knows it or not, the officer on front left third machine has a flat tire.

The officer on the left has been identified as Cary D. Freeman. When Prohibition began, he resigned his position with the police department and joined the Government Alcoholic Tax Unit and was subsequently killed by a bootlegger. The officer on the extreme left has been identified as William Allen. The picture was taken in front of the old Second Precinct Station at the corner of Queen (now Brambleton Avenue) and Lincoln streets. It is no longer in existence. Courtesy of Kirn Memorial Library

In 1913 Alton Tarrall went to work for the engineering department of the city of Norfolk as a rodman. Here he stands on the running board of a 1908 or 1909 Reo, reputed to be the second or third car bought by the city for that department. It was used by W. T. Brooke, city engineer. Mr. Tarrall resigned as a civil engineer in 1966. Courtesy of Alton Tarrall

Before the days of radio and television, when the World Series began both the Virginian-Pilot, *located on Tazewell Street,* and the Ledger-Dispatch *on Plume Street* set up electric scoreboards in front of their respective buildings to give baseball fans a running account of the games. When the games were being played, many an office boy, a clerk, or even the boss disappeared from work for the afternoon. The streets were impassable for vehicular traffic. This scoreboard picture, taken from the October 8, 1913, issue of the Virginian-Pilot, *shows the crowd and board on Tazewell Street.*

All bundled up, this group of young folks is ready to brave the cold in 1914. Courtesy of William L. Tazewell

Four small ferry boats seem to hover like butterflies over the Old Dominion steamer Monroe *as she prepares to dock at the foot of Church Street (now St. Paul Boulevard), a short distance away. The line had a regular daily (except Sundays) passenger and freight service between Norfolk and New York. At this particular time a berth in a minimum-priced stateroom, including three meals, cost ten dollars. Most of its boats were taken over by the government during World War II, and several were sunk. The line never resumed this service. Photograph by Harry C. Mann, 1914; courtesy of Kirn Memorial Library*

A section of Norfolk's waterfront from Berkley taken from a 1914 panoramic picture of Harry C. Mann covers that part of the ferry docks (not shown) on the left to the Old Dominion Steamship Company's piers and warehouses between Church and Nebraska streets, where a number of their vessels are docked. The tall building is the National Bank of Commerce on the corner of Main and Atlantic streets. The church spire is that of St. Mary's Catholic Church on Holt Street. Most of the area in the foreground was totally destroyed by fire in June 1931. The American Peanut Company in the center was one of the buildings lost. It never resumed business in Norfolk. Courtesy of N. H. Bundy, Jr.

Southgate Terminal and Freemason Harbour

Walter H. Taylor III photographed McCullough's Wharf, also known as McCullough's Docks, about 1897. The trestle bridge connects Boush Street with Newton Street (later Boush Street extension). Railway docks and warehouses are in the upper center portion of the picture.

A. A. McCullough, one of Norfolk's most enterprising citizens of the latter part of the nineteenth century, was engaged in the lumber business at the foot of old Church Street (now St. Paul Boulevard). About 1870 he moved his business to the northwest corner of Granby Street and Town Back Creek (later City Hall Avenue), where the old Royster Building now stands. A stone bridge connected North and South Granby Streets as they were sometimes referred to. While most of the creek had been filled in beyond Bank Street, much of it up to the bridge was still open and marshy, often exuding a malodorous stench, especially in warm weather. People constantly complained.

While the stone bridge and marshy area of the creek on the eastern side of the bridge prevented sailing craft from going beyond, as they once had been able to do, they could come up to the west side of the creek, which was not filled in to Boush Street until 1905. McCullough bulkheaded his property on the north side of the creek and built a substantial dock, which became known as McCullough's Wharf or Dock, and was used by watercraft.

A large portion of the area just west of Boush Street, including almost the entire area of the present day Southgate Terminal, was on unsightly, odoriferous, mosquito-ridden marsh land. McCullough reclaimed about sixty-five acres of it, some of which was later sold to the New York, Philadelphia, and Norfolk Railroad (usually referred to as the "Nip-an-N"), later the Pennsylvania Railroad, the Chesapeake and Ohio Railroad, and the Anheuser-Busch Brewing Company. In the early 1880s the two railroads, within a few years of each other, established pier-warehouses on some of the reclaimed land, and Anheuser-Busch put up a one-story building on the southwest corner of Boush Street and Brooke Avenue. The latter street came into existence about 1900. The Norfolk and Western Railroad built a connection from Water Street over the creek and into the area. This connection was discontinued during World War I.

McCullough's reclaimed marsh gained new importance in the new century. Up to the early 1900s most of Norfolk's wholesale and manufacturing businesses, especially groceries, were located on Water Street and adjacent cross streets. About 1914 Thomas S. Southgate, a food broker, conceived the idea of bringing all of the wholesale grocers in Norfolk into one area, enabling them to operate more efficiently and profitably. Southgate envisioned large warehouses served by the Chesapeake and Ohio Railroad. The area selected was McCullough's reclaimed land; the railroad entered into an arrangement with Southgate, and the Southgate Terminal Corporation was formed.

The first row of warehouses on the south side of Tazewell Street from Duke to Dunmore streets was ready by 1915. Shortly afterwards, another section of warehouses was built on the west side of Dunmore Street, ending at present-day College Place. A third section was built at the foot of Tazewell Street and extended several hundred feet beyond the shoreline into the river. There is a story that this warehouse originally was planned to be one story and to extend to the Port Warden's line. A beautiful view of the river at the end of Botetourt and Freemason streets would have been obstructed if such a warehouse were built. Accordingly, Col. Charles Grandy, who lived on the corner, and others protested. Southgate evidently acceded to their protests, trimming the length of the pier and making it two stories instead of one.

This is a 1915 view of the harbor and construction of the new Southgate Terminal. Another section of warehouses will be added to the right, and a new pier-warehouse will also be added to the building under construction. Tracks are being laid to the rear of this building. Atlantic City is in the center, and to the left is the plant of the Anheuser-Busch Brewing Company. Courtesy of Norfolk and Western Railway

A waterfront view of the Southgate Terminal area in 1920. The pier-warehouse of the Southgate Forwarding and Storage Company is on the center left, and across the slip is the pier-warehouse of the Chesapeake and Ohio Railway. Adjoining it is the pier-warehouse of the New York, Philadelphia and Norfolk Railroad (Pennsylvania Railroad). Beyond it on the center right are the warehouses of the Old Bay Line. The white building in the center is the Royster Building on Granby Street.

The pier-warehouse operated by Southgate represented such lines as the North German Lloyd, the Dollar Line, and the American-Hawaiian Steamship Company, whose ships all docked at the pier-warehouse. Photograph by Acme Photo Company; courtesy of Kirn Memorial Library

The Southgate Terminal as shown in 1930. The Southgate complex is the slightly crooked "Y" in the center left. It is served by the C&O Railway Yard. The C&O warehouse is across the slip from the Southgate pier-warehouse. Next to the C&O is the operation of the NYP&N, about half of which was destroyed in the 1933 hurricane and never replaced. The warehouse-piers in the bottom right are those of the Merchants and Miners Transportation Company and the Old Bay Line. Courtesy of Kirn Memorial Library

Change, however subtle, is ever-present. After World War II, a slow decline took place. As business fell off, the two railroads gradually curtailed their operations, and when the Colonial Stores, largest occupant of the terminal, moved their operations to the Industrial Park in the early 1960s, the Southgate terminal was doomed. The two railroads no longer operate in the terminal and the old plant of the Anheuser-Busch Brewing Company (later Boush Cold Storage Company) has been partially destroyed by fire. Its ultimate fate is uncertain, but there are plans to renovate and develop the property with town houses, condominiums, and small shops. The old C&O warehouse-pier is now occupied by

the Norfolk School of Boatbuilding, where the art of boat building is taught. The old car-float slip between the railroad's warehouse and that of the Southgate pier has been deepened and a concrete pier has been built around most of it, making it available for medium-size watercraft. Botetourt Street has been connected with College Place and townhouses have been erected at the corner. Unfortunately, the present economic situation makes the fate of the area at this time rather uncertain.

This 1980 view shows the early stages of development of the new Freemason Harbour-Southgate Terminal area. Townhouses have been built

on College Place and Botetourt Street (center left). College Place once ended at Duke Street since most of the area in the center was marshland, later reclaimed. The two dark-roofed buildings in the center are Southgate warehouses. The left pier is the old Southgate Forwarding and Storage Company. Apartments may be built on this site. The long building on the right is the old pier-warehouse of the C&O Railway, now occupied by the Norfolk School of Boatbuilding. A concrete apron has been added around the pier with steps leading to the water's edge. This work has now been completed, the apron extending to and around the end of the pier. In the upper right are the new small boat piers. Photograph by S. H. Ringo

On November 8, 1914, the twenty-fifth anniversary of the establishment of St. Joseph's colored Catholic parish was appropriately observed with a solemn high mass. Thirty converts, recently baptized, received their first communion that morning and their confirmation that afternoon by the Right Reverend D. J. O'Connell, Bishop of Richmond.

St. Joseph's parish had its beginning in September 1889 at 635 Brewer Street, the convent and chapel all being housed in the residence still in use in the parish in 1914. The first pastor was Father Lawrence O'Connell, uncle of Bishop O'Connell, who was officiating at these exercises.

The first enrollment at the school consisted of eighty pupils in a dilapidated structure which was insufficient to accommodate all of them, so the overflow had to go to the residence at 635 Brewer Street. In May 1893 a new school and chapel were built on Queen Street now Brambleton Avenue and dedicated immediately. This was a substantial brick building.

St. Joseph's was a very active parish, and during the first twenty-five years of its existence it had baptized over 800 people into the Catholic faith. During the same period of time more than 300 children had passed through the school.

In 1925 Father Vincent D. Warren organized a band known as St. Joseph's Academy Band, with Dr. O. J. Bailey as director and instructor. The members of the band purchased their own uniforms by different forms of entertainment and parties, and they raised enough funds to purchase their own instruments. A football team was organized in 1914 and played for many years. The main opponent was Booker T. Washington High School.

About 1932 the church acquired the property of the Cumberland Street Methodist Church on the corner of Freemason and Cumberland streets. It remained there until the redevelopment of the downtown area slated the church for demolition. During the 1960s St. Joseph's Parish was absorbed by St. Mary's Parish.

The insets in the picture show the original chapel and school on Queen Street (Brambleton Avenue) and St. Joseph's Band. Pictures courtesy of Venetia Grant, now in her seventies, who went to the school and attended services in the chapel. Large photograph by Harry C. Mann

Many will remember the old Strand Theatre located on the west side of Granby Street between College Place and Freemason Street. First class moving pictures were usually shown, but stage plays were occasionally billed there. The theatre was opened in 1914 and closed about 1935. Hofheimer's now occupies the site. Courtesy of Norfolk Historical Society

This picture, taken about 1914, shows delivery boys lined up outside the Postal Telegraph-Cable Company on the southwest corner of Commerce and East Main streets. The company ceased to operate after 1945. Courtesy of J. B. Denney, Jr.

About 1915, the family of Col. Walter H. Taylor II gathered for a picture at their summer home in Blue Ridge Summitt, Pennsylvania. The colonel was aide-de-camp to Gen. Robert E. Lee during the War Between the States. He sits in the center of the group while his wife, "Miss Betty," is just to his left. Three generations are represented in this group.

During the war Mrs. Taylor, the former Elizabeth Selden Saunders, was engaged to Colonel Taylor when Richmond fell. Realizing that the city must be evacuated, Taylor sent her a message to meet him at a friend's house in Richmond with the rector of St. Paul's Episcopal Church at midnight to be married, having received permission from General Lee to take time off to do so. The ceremony was performed sometime after midnight of April 3, 1865, while the city was burning and being evacuated. After the ceremony, Taylor rejoined General Lee and continued on to Appomattox. One week later he returned to Richmond and brought his bride back to Norfolk in a buggy.

After the war, Colonel Taylor was engaged in the hardware business, and later he became president of the Marine Bank of Norfolk. He died in 1916. Courtesy of Janet F. Taylor

Parked in front of Doumar's Confectionery in the Wells Theatre Building on Tazewell Street are members of the Doumar family and their 1914 Studebaker. Left to right are Ralph Absi, an in-law, John, George, and Charles Doumar. It was George Doumar who began selling ice cream cones at Ocean View in 1915 and who opened Doumar's Drive-in on Monticello Avenue in 1934. Courtesy of Al and Vic Doumar

In 1916 that part of Granby Street running north beyond its intersection with Lakewood Drive towards Ward's Corner looked like this. Over the years Granby Street had been gradually extended from downtown Norfolk to Lavalette Avenue (City Park boundary); from Lavalette Avenue and beyond it was known as the Indian Poll Bridge Road, deriving its name from the Indian Pole Bridge that spanned Tanner's Creek (Lafayette river). Although there are several variations of the origin of the name Indian Pole Bridge, none can be verified.

This photograph, taken by Harry C. Mann, appeared in the Virginian-Pilot for April 3, 1916, together with several other similar pictures showing the deplorable condition of the toll roads leading into Norfolk, and calling for improvement. No doubt the 1916 Model T Ford bogged down in the mud gave emphasis to this condition. The picture was taken probably several hundred yards north of the present intersection traffic lights.

In 1923 this part of Norfolk County was annexed by Nofolk, and many gradual changes were made. The streetcar tracks were those of the Bay Shore Line, which ran from downtown to Ocean View. Streetcar service stopped around 1950. In the widening of Granby Street, the tracks were replaced by a center parkway. The creek on the left has been filled in and the houseboats are gone. After the annexation in 1923, the name Indian Pole Bridge Road was replaced by a continuation of Granby Street. 1916 picture courtesy of Betty Williams. The picture of Granby Street in 1980 was taken by Carroll Walker.

Ever to bring a thrill to his public, Buffalo Bill (Col. William F.) Cody, made his last appearance in Norfolk on October 16, 1916. Although the train bringing his show to Norfolk was in a wreck a couple of days before near Victoria, Virginia, killing thirty-three horses, and although Cody was shaken up somewhat, the show went on, beginning with a parade in the morning. A show to be held the previous day in Portsmouth had been cancelled.

The Virginian-Pilot for October 16 reports that performances were given to capacity crowds. A story was told that some Cody fans were given the rare privilege of shaking hands with him at the fair grounds. The following day, and for many days after, they were the envy of all their classmates. The last report was that their hands went unwashed for days.

Cody went south after leaving Norfolk. He had planned to winter in Norfolk but changed his plans and went to Colorado. He died in Denver in January 1917.

When Earl T. Gresham (in straw hat on left) came to Norfolk in 1916, horse-drawn wagons were the accepted mode of transportation for all commodities. With a war in full sway in Europe he sensed an opportunity.

Gresham sold his automobile and used the proceeds as a down payment on one of the area's first motor trucks. This picture, taken in 1919 by Harry C. Mann, shows how Gresham's

original one-man operation had grown to a fleet of nineteen trucks. Today it has diversified into four fields: hauling and rigging, crane service, construction, and maintenance
Courtesy of Earl T. Gresham, Jr.

The winter of 1917-18 was bitterly cold, and freezing temperatures were commonplace. On December 31 the temperature reached a high of 16 degrees and a low of 9 degrees. The Elizabeth River was filled with ice, the Eastern and Southern branches were frozen solid, and much of the James River was frozen. Some intrepid person solved the problem of transportation with a horse and sleigh in Commercial Place. A few days later, on January 5, another blizzard struck Norfolk, adding further to the city's miseries. *Courtesy of Kirn Memorial Library*

This is an unusual picture of the Norfolk Light Artillery Blues mounted on West Freemason Street between Yarmouth and Duke streets. It is believed to have been taken just before the Blues left for the Mexican border in 1916 when Pancho Villa was raiding along the border. *Courtesy of Jean Wallace*

The armory of the Norfolk Light Artillery Blues, Hampton Boulevard. Built in 1914, it was demolished in 1966 after the Blues moved to their new quarters on Virginia Beach Boulevard. The Technology Building of Old Dominion University now stands in its place. Photograph by Carroll Walker

When the Kronprinz Wilhelm and the Prinz Eitel Friedrich, two German raiders of World War I, were chased into the Chesapeake Bay in 1915 by Allied warships, they were subsequently interned at the Norfolk Navy Yard. The internees had much freedom, and to make use of their time, they were given permission to use scrap materials adjacent to their dock. With this scrap they built for themselves a miniature German village, complete with church and fire station. When war was declared by the United States on Germany in April 1917, the ships were confiscated and the men made prisoners. This picture shows some of the men from the Kronprinz Wilhelm making toy soldiers, which they were allowed to sell. Photograph from the National Archives

After their seizure by the United States when war was declared in April 1917, the interned German raiders were converted to army transports. The Kronprinz Wilhelm *was renamed the* George Washington *and the* Prinz Eitel Friedrich *the* von Steuben *after the Prussian officer who tendered his services to George Washington during the Revolution. On her first trip to France in October 1917, the* von Steuben *carried the 3rd Battalion of the 6th Marine Regiment and a group of young officers, shown here, ordered to report for casual duty with the 5th Marine Regiment then in France. In this picture, bottom row, third from left, is Lt. J. Addison Hagan, not long graduated from the Virginia Military Institute, then of Richmond but later of Norfolk. He is "shaking hands" with a police dog. Some months later Lieutenant Hagan was in Belleau Wood, where he rescued a wounded Marine sergeant, returning with him under a terrific fire. For this he received a distinguished service medal and a lengthy citation. A few days later he was wounded in the hip while charging across a wheat field with his outfit and was left with a permanent limp.*

Hagan came to Norfolk in 1924 and operated a building material business. When the Marine Corps called for retired officers in 1944, he re-entered, serving in the Pacific as a member of Admiral Halsey's headquarters staff. The inset picture was taken while Colonel Hagan was on Halsey's staff. Returning to Norfolk, Hagan engaged in politics and later won a seat in the Virginia House of Delegates. Always busy, he gradually collected eleven larger-than-life marble statues of famous artists sculpted by Moses Ezekiel, also a graduate of the Virginia Military Institute, which he presented to the city of Norfolk. They are now located in Norfolk's Botanical gardens. Colonel Hagan passed away in 1980. Courtesy of J. A. Hagan, Jr.

126

It is 1917 and the United States is engaged in war. These three pictures show soldiers, sailors, and marines parading on East Main Street in the vicinity of Commerce Street. Courtesy of Kirn Memorial Library

During World War I Harry C. Mann took this photo of a crowded East Main Street near the corner of Commerce Street. Servicemen are highly visible. The automobiles in the center, commonly called jitney buses, are the forerunners of a new form of transportation—the bus. Photo by Harry C. Mann

Fort Story at Cape Henry came into existence in 1917 when it was decided to erect a fort at that point for the protection of the Chesapeake Bay and the cities in the Hampton Roads area. Taken in 1924 by H. D. Vollmer, this picture shows the big guns in target practice at the fort.

128

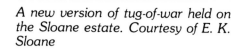

A new version of tug-of-war held on the Sloane estate. Courtesy of E. K. Sloane

During World War I, William Sloane and his wife, Florence K. Sloane, often entertained servicemen. On weekends they would gather several hundred men from the Navy "Y" on Brooke Avenue and transport them to their estate in Lochhaven on Tanner's Creek (Elizabeth River). Sandwiches and drinks were served, and various sporting events were held.

This photo shows about 300 or 400 men at the Sloanes'. Mrs. Sloane, in white, is standing in the center, in front of some British sailors in dark uniforms. Mr. Sloane is seated on her left. Their two children, Edward and William, are standing at left of the group. Courtesy of E. K. Sloane

Commercial Place as it appeared in 1920. Originally called "the road that leadeth to the water," later The Parade, Market Square, and Commercial Place, it was the hub of Norfolk's business life for 250 years. This picture was taken by the Acme Photo Company from Water Street, now a part of Waterfront Drive.

The week of June 23 to July 1, 1919, was designated by the city as Welcome Home Week, a celebration for local men returning from France. A week of festivities was planned, with racing, dancing, and fireworks—culminating in a Grand Mardi Gras Ball on the Hague Saturday night and the coronation of a king and queen of the festival. Between 30,000 and 50,000 people were expected to attend.

At the appointed hour of the coronation, Mayor Albert Roper had requested that "every steam whistle, every factory whistle and horn ashore and afloat blow at 9:00 p.m. Homing pigeons as doves of peace were to be released while the bells of nearby Christ Church would ring loudly as the king and queen, who were to float up the Hague on a white barge to the Sunken Gardens take their place for the coronation." The accompanying photograph shows King John and Queen Pauline awaiting the crowning. After the coronation and some specialty entertainment, Mowbray Arch was turned over to dancing.

There is a story that at the rehearsal for the coronation the day before at the Armory Building, the newly elected director of public safety, retired Rear-Admiral Dillingham, "while going to his office in a hurry happened to glance into the armory, where he saw the king's stately figure—legs and all," attired in his Elizabethan costume, performing the necessary evolutions pertinent to the coronation." The admiral, when he took office, had announced his intentions to "clean up Norfolk"; therefore, he rushed to his office and dictated the following letter:

"To those in charge of the Red Circle Theatre, Armory Building: Will you please see that the gentleman, who is prancing around the armory hall, not fully attired, will please put on enough clothes not to make him objectionable to the public."

The "gentleman" was State Senator John Lesner. The item rated a headline in the following day's paper. Courtesy of Norfolk Historical Society

The new Virginia National Bank Building built in 1963 is located on Main Street and the upper part of what was formerly Commercial Place. This picture was taken from the lower part of Commercial Place where the ferries once docked and now occupied by the Omni International Hotel. Photograph by Carroll Walker, 1980

The second city market (also known as the Armory and the Municipal Building), located on City Hall Avenue between Brewer Street and Monticello Avenue, was long a landmark in downtown Norfolk. The building was erected about 1892 as the city began to expand, and a better market site was needed when the first market in Market Square (Commercial Place) had outlived its usefulness. The Maritime Tower now stands in its place.

In addition to functioning as a market, the building housed city offices, and local militia companies also had quarters there. A large auditorium in the building served many purposes: a drill hall for the militia, a place for large meetings and banquets, and a hall for various kinds of entertainment. The Norfolk Symphony held its first concert there about 1920, and Will Rogers and others also entertained there.

Sometime after 1900 additions were made in the rear of the market by the erection of two long shed-like structures to take care of increasing business. About 1923 these buildings were torn down and a new stone market erected in their place. Both structures came down when the Maritime Tower was built in 1954. On the left is the Monticello Hotel and in the distance the old gas tanks. Photograph by Hall Optical Company, 1920

133

This 1979 picture shows the change in the old market area. The Monticello Hotel and the Dickson Building (behind the hotel) were demolished to make way for a new Federal Building. Dominion National Bank and the Maritime Tower stand on the site of the old market building. Photograph by Carroll Walker

Built on the site of an extension of the 1893 wooden city market on Monticello Avenue, a new stone market building was erected in 1923 and was considered one of the best of its kind in the south. This is a rare picture of the interior of one section of the market taken about 1935. Many people will recall in particular the excellent meats of R. M. Eastwood and Company, whose place of business is shown on the left side. The inset shows the stone market. Courtesy of Kirn Memorial Library

This is a rare view taken in 1920 from the old Union Station Building of East Main Street looking towards Church Street (now St. Paul Boulevard). The building in the lower right with the turret-like top is on the corner of East Street, about a block long, and one of the first streets laid out in 1680-81. Main Street turned slightly left in the center at Church. The many-windowed building in the center was the old Gladstone Hotel on Nebraska Street. Built before the turn of the century, it was a popular hotel but became "tarnished" in later years and was eventually taken over by the Union Mission. The two tall buildings are the National Bank of Commerce (now First and Merchants National Bank) on the left and the Royster Building in the upper center right. *Photograph by Acme Photo Company*

This 1922 view is probably the earliest known aerial photo of the old Union Station located at the foot of East Main Street. It was built in 1912 to house the headquarters of the Norfolk and Portsmouth Belt Line Railroad, the Virginian Railway, and the Norfolk Southern Railroad. The Norfolk and Western Railway, with headquarters in Roanoke, Virginia, maintained a general superintendent's office in the building. All used the station for their trains except the Belt Line, which was engaged in a switching service.

In 1963 the building was demolished, the tracks pulled up, and the site converted to other purposes. A portion of the new Waterfront Drive runs through the upper center of this picture, connecting with Tidewater Drive and the Virginia Beach Expressway. The inset picture shows one of the spacious waiting rooms of the station.

When Norfolk was first surveyed in 1680, most of this area was under water, first known as Dun-in-the-Mire, Newton's Creek and Mahone's Lake, extending westerly to Church Street (now St. Paul Boulevard). It was gradually filled in over the years, and the only remaining vestige of it appears in the upper right as a canal. *Courtesy of Curtis Mills*

In 1920 the controversial Brig. Gen. William "Billy" Mitchell, assistant chief of staff of the U.S. Air Force, persuaded the army to buy the airship Roma from the Italian government. At 140 feet long, the Roma was the largest semi-rigid airship ever built, built in Italy after World War I. The ship was dismantled in sections and shipped to Langley Field, Virginia, arriving in August 1921 for reassembly. Here the Roma hovers over Granby and Tazewell streets in 1921. Courtesy of Kirn Memorial Library

The Roma seemed to be beset with trouble from the beginning. The air bag was discovered to be filled with mildew; the engines failed to warm up during an early flight; engine troubles caused cancellations and delays in flights.

During a southward flight over Hampton Roads and Norfolk on February 21, 1922, some trouble was experienced as the dirigible passed the Army Base, and a decision was made to attempt a forced landing. At this time the nose caved in, jamming the controls, and the Roma dropped rapidly to less than 1,000 feet from the depot below.

As the Roma descended, efforts to control it failed. The crew threw out everything possible in order to lighten it. But as the dirigible reached the ground it struck high voltage wires on telephone poles, and the hydrogen and gas tanks instantly exploded. Less than thirty minutes since it had left Langley Field, the Roma crashed. Thirty-four people perished. Courtesy of Kirn Memorial Library

A Navy recruiting team—band, torpedo, and all—pauses for a few minutes to let a photographer take a picture of its activity in 1920. The scene is in front of the Confederate Monument at the head of Commercial Place. The building behind the monument is the department store of W. G. Swartz and Company, formerly Miller, Rhoads & Swartz. Courtesy of C. S. Barrett

The First Baptist Church on the corner of Westover and Moran avenues as it appeared in 1920. This was the first Baptist church in Norfolk. Organized in 1805 with help from a Baptist church in Portsmouth, it was interracial. Later the congregation separated, the blacks forming the First Baptist Church on Bute Street and the whites erecting a church on Cumberland and Market streets, known as the Cumberland Street Baptist Church. In 1848 some of the membership of the Cumberland church formed the Freemason Street Baptist Church, giving Norfolk three Baptist churches.

In 1886 the Cumberland Street Baptist Church became the First Baptist Church of Norfolk. This building was sold in 1895 and the recently vacated structure of the Granby Street Methodist Church on Granby and Freemason Streets purchased, the latter Church becoming the Epworth Methodist Church. In 1910 the First Baptist moved to Moran and Westover Avenues in Ghent. This building was destroyed by fire on October 2, 1970. In 1974 a new building was occupied on the Kempsville Road. Courtesy Kirn Memorial Library

In 1921 Barney Lifland operated a small grocery store on the corner of Voss and Queen (now Brambleton Avenue) streets between Boush and Granby streets. The store was known as Barney's Market. A picture taken in 1921 shows the exterior of his store and his two children. The interior is shown in the insert.

In the middle 1930s the Norfolk Newspapers, in an expansion program, acquired the site of Barney's Market and additional property westward for the erection of a new building for their increased activities, displacing Barney's. On October 28, 1937, the new building was formally dedicated. Barney's Market was originally located on the left side of the entrance to the building. Courtesy of Kirn Memorial Library

The Ocean View Volunteer Fire Department, 1922.

OCEAN VIEW VOLUNTEER FIRE Dept 1922
GAUGHAN

This aerial view of the downtown waterfront was taken in 1922 before it began to decline. On the left is the Cape Charles boat of the Pennsylvania Railroad. Next to it are the warehouses and piers of the Merchants and Miners Transportation Company. The line had a tri-weekly freight and passenger service to Boston. In the lower center is a steamer of the Old Bay Line, which had a daily service to and from Baltimore. Around the side on the right was the warehouse slip of the Chesapeake Steamship Company, also maintaining a daily service to Baltimore. A little above the center right is a steamer of the Old Dominion Line, which had a regular daily service to New York City. In addition, there were other small boat lines using the piers. The street on the right is Water Street, where most manufacturing and wholesale houses were. To the left of it is Main Street. Everything below Water Street has since been torn down. Photograph courtesy of Curtis Mills

After the growth of Ghent in the 1890-1900 period, Norfolk suddenly seemed to expand in all directions: Colonial Place, Larchmont, Lochaven, and other sections. This aerial view of the North Shore Point-Algonquin Park area on the north side of the Lafayette River adjacent to Hampton Boulevard was taken about 1923, and it has developed into a section of well-landscaped grounds and beautiful homes. The curved road in the upper center is North Shore Road. Courtesy of Norfolk Historical Society

A 1923 view of Hampton Boulevard (then Myers Avenue) looking north from between Forty-sixth and Forty-seventh streets. Not visible in the picture is Gray's Pharmacy a business started in 1918 on the corner of Forty-eighth and Myers Avenue and a landmark in the area, partially hidden by the trees on the right. Courtesy of Kirn Memorial Library

The same view in 1980. Part of the campus of Old Dominion University, started in 1930, is seen on the left. Gray's Pharmacy, still in operation, is at the end of the block of stores on the right. When this area was annexed by Norfolk in 1923, the name Myers Avenue was changed to Hampton Boulevard. Photograph by Carroll Walker

In 1925 a group of city and Ford Motor Company officials and local businessmen gather around the first automobile to come off the assembly line of the new Ford Motor Company plant. Leaning on the left side of the car is Mayor S. Heth Tyler. Courtesy of Kirn Memorial Library

Unknown to many and only vaguely remembered by a few is the fact that Norfolk at one time had a polo team. It was composed of members of the Norfolk Light Artillery Blues, Norfolk's oldest military unit dating back to 1829.

This picture was taken behind the old Blues Armory on West Forty-seventh Street about 1924. The polo team was formed while the Blues were at their annual summer training in Tobyhana, Pennsylvania, in 1924. They played among themselves or with other teams in the Tidewater area, such as Grime's Battery in Portsmouth. According to an item in the Virginian-Pilot for June 16, 1924, the blues won a match with the Service Battery, 111th Field Artillery, Virginia National Guard, Newport News.

On the team were Lieutenant Colonel William H. Sands, 111th Field Artillery, Virginia National Guard, and Judge R. B. Spindle, Jr., of Norfolk. One of the members of the team, Capt. Ira B. White (the hatless man sixth from left) stated that when they first started playing at Tobyhana they used broomsticks stuck in croquet mallets. The team went out of existence about 1927.

Ever since it was formed, the Women's Auxiliary of the old Norfolk Protestant Hospital, later the Norfolk General Hospital, held an annual fund-raising project such as a play. In 1924 they produced a musical called "Egyptian Nights of 1924." One of the scenes was called "The Parade of the Wooden Soldiers," which, no doubt, was inspired by a song of the same name in a musical in New York at that time, the participants being dressed as wooden soldiers. Those performing locally were well known. Left to right, sitting: Davis W. Jordan, Walter H. Taylor III, James Iredell Jenkins, Capt. William B. Baldwin, and Nathan H. Bundy. Standing: Moran Barry, W. W. Old, Jr., Louis Dobie, John S. Jenkins, Arthur Stansbury, and W. Ludwell Baldwin. Courtesy of Kirn Memorial Library

As a publicity stunt, a writer of the old Ledger-Dispatch in November 1924 conceived the idea of having a modern day couple live in a dense woods for a week, as primitively as possible, with no possessions of any kind on their persons, and dressed just adequately to protect themselves from exposure or injury. Volunteers were asked for.

A young couple volunteered and were accepted when they agreed to get married for the occasion. The marriage took place the morning of November 12 in the window of The Hub Clothing Store, then located on the present site of the Trailways Bus Terminal on East Main Street. Bride Floretta Popejoy's wedding gown was a loose-fitting, heavy piece of cloth wrapped around her body, no stockings, and heavy shoes. Groom Robert J. Day wore a heavy woolen sweater, heavy trousers, and shoes. More than 5,000 people crowded the street in front of the window.

The couple were taken to a densely wooden area known only to those connected with the affair and then were left to their own devices. A reporter and photographer would contact them secretly each day. For a week they subsisted on the land as well as possible. Their first "home" of tree limbs and branches collapsed, but a dugout with a bed of leaves and grass in the side of an embankment was more substantial. It was difficult to remain warm at night. At times an

extra fire was built in a depression. When the ground was warm enough, they would brush the ashes aside and sleep there, covering themselves with moss and leaves. One night was so cold they covered themselves with sand and dirt. Their meals consisted mainy of fruits berries, and nuts. A few rabbits were trapped. The man made a bow and arrow at one time, but it was not very effective. Water was kept in a hollow log.

The Days were "rescued" the following week by, left to right: unknown, Lt. A. M. Harrison, Jacob "Abe" Leon, and C. E. Wright. The couple spent several days making public appearances and receiving gifts donated by merchants and others. Photograph by H. D. Vollmer

These 1925 Packards are lined up in front of the Seaboard Air Line Railway Building (now Wainwright Building) on Bute Street with their ostensible owners presumably waiting to go somewhere. Courtesy of Merritt J. Horne

In 1925 Norfolk's waterfront and downtown area looked like this. The picture takes in the area from the foot of Church Street (St. Paul Boulevard), where the docks of the Old Dominion Steamship Company were located in the lower center, to the Hague and Mowbray Arch in Ghent in the upper right. The cluster of buildings in the center are the National Bank of Commerce and Board of Trade Building; above it the Monticello Hotel and off center left the Royster Building. The Southgate Terminal complex is just above the Royster Building.

This picture shows about the same area in April 1980. Extensive change has taken place in the downtown area. Waterfront Drive, a new thoroughfare connecting with the Virginia Beach Expressway on one end and Boush Street-Brambleton Avenue on the other, eliminated most of Water Street. The new Virginia National Bank (formerly the National Bank of Commerce) stands at Main Street and the upper part of old Commercial Place, dominating the area. Across from it in the lower center is the Omni International Hotel, covering the entire waterfront area where the ferry docks were once located. Only two small buildings (center left) remain of the many small buildings, which once characterized this area.

The upper part of the picture shows (left) the Atlantic City area, Medical Tower (center), a part of Ghent and the Hague Tower on Mowbray Arch. The Southgate Terminal complex, now undergoing renovation, is in the upper center just below the Medical Tower. *Photograph by S. H. Ringo*

In the days before television and radio, first-hand information about a World Series was provided by the Ledger-Dispatch and the Virginian-Pilot on their scoreboards in front of their respective buildings on Plume Street and Tazewell Street. This crowd of baseball fans gathered in the late 1920s in front of the scoreboard of the Ledger-Dispatch on Plume Street. *Courtesy of Abe Goldblatt*

The Norfolk and Western Grain Elevator at Sewell's Point as it appeared in 1925. *Courtesy of Chamber of Commerce*

144

The First Church of Christ, Scientist, West Freemason Street, as it appeared in 1927. Its first reading room was held in a part of the old George Newton house on the southwest corner of College Place and Granby Street in 1896. When the Second Presbyterian Church, which built this structure, moved to a new location in 1903 on Yarmouth Street, the First Church of Christ, Scientist, acquired the building. In the 1960s the church moved to a new location on Granby Street. The building pictured is now used by the International Order of Odd Fellows. Photograph by Acme; courtesy of Kirn Memorial Library

A 1925 photograph of the Norfolk and Western freight yards at the foot of East Main Street. The dark building in the center is the N&W grain elevator which burned in 1941. Courtesy of Chamber of Commerce

Beauty contests were often held at Ocean View, and 1927 was no different from any other year. Courtesy of Norfolk Historical Society

In 1929, Ben Epstein, a World War I pilot and airplane parts-scrap dealer began an air taxi service between Norfolk and Richmond from a small airfield on the northwest side of Granby Street and Taussig Boulevard. He called his operation the Grand Central Airport Terminal and later Norfolk Airport, Inc. Many people will recall the one-story stucco building which was Epstein's administration building and which was torn down in the 1980s. The Luddington Line, an airline of the late twenties, operated a daily passenger service from there to Washington, D.C., and later Eastern Air Lines used the field for a Norfolk-Richmond service. Epstein desired to expand his operations in 1932 but was strongly opposed by the Navy because of the closeness of the field to Navy's operations. As a result of this, the Ludington Line and the Eastern Air Line moved their operations to the Glen Rock Airport on the Virginia Beach Boulevard. The Navy finally acquired the property in 1940. Courtesy of Kirn Memorial Library

Granby Street between Market and Freemason streets in 1929 was a busy place. Rice's at that time was located on both sides of the Norva Theatre. In a few years it would move to the Y.M.C.A. building on the corner of Freemason and Granby streets and later to the Ames and Brownley building across the street. Courtesy of Kirn Memorial Library

Years
of
Change

1930~1960

This 1930 photograph shows the intersection now known as Ward's Corner. When the picture was taken the area was practically all farmland. The name came into existence when A. C. Ward, who operated a grocery store and Texaco service station on the northwest corner of Sewell's Point Road (now Little Creek Road— running from center right to upper left)

and Granby Street (crossing Sewell's Point Road on the right), was appointed a Michelin tire dealer. The tire company representative placed signs on converging roads reading: "Mr. Ward wants to see you at Ward's Corner"—and the name stuck.

Ward's station is the white building with gray overhanging roof, just right of center. Tegg's Log Cabin is across

the street (roof in two sections, one gray, one black).

The aerial view of the same area was taken from an opposite angle and shows how much Ward's Corner had developed by 1963. The building in the lower center (with white triangle on the roof) is Hofheimer's, formerly the site of Tegg's Log Cabin. Courtesy of Mrs. J. Buell Tegg

Across from Ward's tire dealership J. Buell Tegg and his brother, Herbert, operated a Standard Oil station and a small restaurant called Tegg's Log Cabin, reputed to be the first in Norfolk to specialize in barbecue. The business grew rapidly from its 1929 beginning, and around 1934 a larger building was erected (above). The restaurant was torn down in the 1940s and Hofheimer's is on the site now. Courtesy of Mrs. J. Buell Tegg

What did many Norfolk people do on Easter Sunday in March 1930? They went to a grand Easter Day parade held at Virginia Beach to observe the newest styles. Apparently it was a little too chilly that day to enjoy the full benefit of the parade. Courtesy of Kirn Memorial Library

The A. C. Cox Grocery Company began business on the corner of Bank Street and City Hall Avenue in 1930 and ceased operations in 1955. Courtesy of Kirn Memorial Library

The new Kirn Memorial Library was constructed on City Hall Avenue between Atlantic and Bank streets and a part of Plume Street in 1964. It displaced the A. C. Cox Grocery which had been on the northeast corner since 1930. Courtesy of Kirn Memorial Library

This was once a residence on the southwest corner of Boush and Charlotte streets, but by the time of this 1930s photograph its lower part had been converted to stores. The building was removed in the 1960s, and the Bank of the Commonwealth now occupies the site. Photograph by H. D. Vollmer

About 1930 Rice's moved into a new location on the southeast corner of Granby and Freemason streets in a building formerly occupied by the Y.M.C.A., where they remained until about 1938 when they moved into their present location, which building had been occupied by Ames and Brownley. This picture was taken in the summer of 1932 when the Depression was at its worst. Note that Rices was then advertising fur coats for $55, which doesn't seem to attract the group of women gazing at perhaps a better bargain in the other window. And perhaps the ragged little newsboy is having trouble selling his papers, although they were selling for 3¢ a copy at that time. Courtesy of Kirn Memorial Library

In March 1930 the city began to widen Boush Street. The area shown here is between Freemason and Bute streets, looking north. On the left are the Boush Street school and the Medical Arts Building. On the right a part of the Epworth Methodist Church can be seen. The buildings beyond the church are mostly homes that are either being converted into stores or waiting to be torn down, including the three-story house in the center of the picture.

A 1932 view of the Towne Point area of downtown Norfolk looking west. The vessel in the picture is the George Washington, which had been undergoing repairs at the Navy Yard in Portsmouth. Courtesy of Kirn Memorial Library

On August 23, 1933, Norfolk was hit by one of the worst hurricanes in its history. The water rose nine feet over mean tide, completely inundating all low-lying areas in the city. This scene shows the area along Mowbray Arch and Mill Street in the Ghent section of Norfolk when the Hague overflowed its banks. The girls are standing on the sidewalk, and the automobile, which is actually parked on the far side of Mowbray Arch, is almost covered. *Courtesy of Kirn Memorial Library*

Dress parade at the Naval Operating Base, Norfolk, Virginia, August 1935. It has been estimated that more than 50 percent of all naval recruits trained during World War I were trained at this base. These men are from the electricians' school. Behind them in the U.S.S. Electrician, *the ship that never went to sea. This was a training ship used at the base in the 1920s and '30s. Courtesy of C. S. Barrett*

In 1934 a small airport known as the Granby Street Airport was established on Granby Street. One observer described it as "made of tar paper, scrap lumber, wire stays—and a prayer to hold it together." John L. Gore was the field manager. The planes on the field are, left to right: Boeing 247 Transport (Luddington Air Lines), Aeronca C-3, two place trainer aircraft, Bellanca-Cabin 5 place private. Flights were made over the area, and the Luddington line flew to Washington, D. C.

This curve was formerly called "dead man's curve" because of many accidents which occurred there. Today the site is a healing center, the location of DePaul Hospital. Photograph by James W. Croom

From 1636 to 1955 there was always a regular ferry service of some kind between Norfolk and Portsmouth and later Berkley—from a hand-rowed skiff in 1636 to one such as the Rockaway pictured here in 1935. After the Berkley Bridge-Tunnel was built in 1954, the ferry service stopped forever. Courtesy of Kirn Memorial Library

In 1935 the Norfolk Southern Railroad inaugurated a rail-bus service from Norfolk to Virginia Beach. This picture shows a regular bus connecting with the rail bus at the Norfolk Southern Park Avenue connection. The service was discontinued in 1948. Courtesy of Kirn Memorial Library

In 1936 Daniel K. Ludwig, who was in the cargo ship business, came to Norfolk with an idea that revolutionized that business and founded the Welding Shipyard on Hampton Boulevard near the Naval Base. Here he developed the technique of welding, rather than riveting, seagoing vessels. At the same time he conceived the idea of launching sideways of cargo ships. He also developed the concept of the supertankers here. The accompanying photograph from the 1940s shows one of his ships being launched —sideways, of course.

In 1951 Ludwig moved his shipbuilding operations to Kure, Japan, to take advantage of cheap labor there and build bigger tankers. Since then he has built tankers as large as 200,000 tons. The Welding Shipyard still operates here, but it is now a division of the National Bulk Carriers. Ludwig is now embarked on a massive tree growing operation in Brazil. Photograph by H. D. Vollmer

This is not an imitation of New Year's Eve in Times Square but the beginning of the Christmas season in Norfolk for 1937. In those days merchants did not rush the Christmas season by displaying their goods in August or September; they waited until after Thanksgiving. At 7:30 p.m., December 6, 1937, as planned by the downtown merchants, Granby Street from Freemason Street to City Hall Avenue became ablaze with lights, ushering in the Christmas season for that year. Three bands were playing, one at Freemason Street, the Fireman's Band in front of Smith and Welton on College Place, and the other at City Hall Avenue. This picture shows the crowd in front of Smith and Welton. Courtesy of Kirn Memorial Library

On February 6, 1936, the Norfolk area was visited by one of its worst snowstorms in years. Most business closed down. The cold was severe along the eastern seaboard. The Baltimore-Washington area reported the Potomac River as having ice from bank to bank between nine and eighteen inches thick, causing the cancellation of all bay steamers. Although ice filled the Elizabeth River and Hampton Roads, boats were still able to navigate. This picture shows the Chesapeake and Ohio Railroad steamer Virginia, surrounded by ice, on its regular run carrying passengers and mail from Newport News to Norfolk. The steamer was a familiar sight on the river and was usually called Smokey Joe. It was reported to be one of the fastest steamers of its kind in the area. The C&O terminated its steamer service in 1949, and in 1950 Smokey Joe made its last trip—towed to Baltimore and broken up for junk. Photograph by H. D. Vollmer

In a section of Norfolk that has completely disappeared were small, diversified businesses such as Hiram A. Miller's modest fish market, located on the corner of Fenchurch and Cove streets, catering specifically to the wants and needs of people living in the immediate area. One of his specialties, as advertised on the front of his store, was muskrats, often referred to as "marsh rabbits." Considered a delicacy, they were caught mainly by trapping. In 1937 their hides brought between $1.25 and $2.50 each. Photograph by H. D. Vollmer

Saturday afternoon on Granby Street at the intersection of College Place-Market Street as the Christmas season of 1936 approached. Photograph by H. D. Vollmer

The Morning Room features this painting by Epson of Florence K. Sloane. Photograph by Carroll Walker

The Hermitage Museum is located in this Tudor-style building in the Lochaven section on the Lafayette River. Organized in 1937 by William Sloane and Florence K. Sloane, his wife, the museum displays artwork from all over the world in galleries paneled and carved in oak, walnut, and teak. The Far East collection is of special interest. Photograph by Carroll Walker

The collection in the Great Hall is
varied. Hand-carved witches deco-
rate each side of the fireplaces at both
ends of the room. Photograph by
Carroll Walker

Altschul's on Church Street was a popular department store which ran from Church to Cumberland Street. The inset picture shows the original store, which was first opened by Benjamin Altschul at 534-36 Church Street in 1898 and moved to the location shown in this 1938 picture in June 1910. The business was sold in the '70s, the new owners moving to Granby Street. Although not in use at this time, the old building still stands, the last old Church Street building. The interior picture was taken by Harry C. Mann in 1915. Courtesy of Mrs. Herbert Altschul and Benjamin Altschul

Looking north on Church Street from City Hall Avenue as it appeared in 1939. This part of Church Street has disappeared entirely, replaced by St. Paul Boulevard in the 1960s. The trees on the left are located in the churchyard of old St. Paul's Church, which is still standing. The only other building still standing in 1981 is Altschul's department store, upper center. The building was sold sometime ago and the business moved to Granby Street, the Altschuls having retired.

Snyder's Department Store on Church Street between Plume Street and City Hall Avenue was one of the old popular stores of its kind in that section of Norfolk. Begun about 1905, it continued into the 1960s until the redevelopment of the area necessitated its closing down. This picture was taken in the late 1930s. Courtesy of Kirn Memorial Library

On July 17, 1938, an Irishman by the name of Douglas Corrigan took off from the Floyd Bennett Field Airport in Brooklyn, New York, in a "third hand" airplane. He flew alone, without any so-called necessary costly instruments, presumably bound for California, but twenty-four hours later he landed in Ireland. When questioned on his arrival there, Corrigan claimed he had become lost in some manner and had missed California. For this he was dubbed "Wrong Way" Corrigan.

When Corrigan returned to the United States sometime later, he was greeted as a conquering hero and commenced a tour of the country, which included Norfolk. He arrived here on August 30, 1938, being duly greeted by city officials and crowds of people wherever he went. A banquet and dance were given in his honor at the Nansemond Hotel. The photograph shown here was taken by Charles Borjes of the Virginian-Pilot at the Glen Rock Airport. Corrigan is presumably explaining to Mayor Gurkin (right) how he got lost and wound up in Ireland. Courtesy of John A. Gurkin, Jr.

While playing at the Cavalier Hotel on Labor Day weekend in September 1939, Charles "Buddy" Rogers, actor, orchestra leader, and husband of Mary Pickford, was suddenly taken ill and was forced to retire to his room at the hotel. Miss Pickford, who was in California at the time and who was slated to be in South Boston, Virginia, on September 7 to be crowned queen of the twenty-fifth annual Tobacco Festival, immediately flew to Norfolk, where she was met by Mayor John A. Gurkin, Frank Turin of the advertising board, W. S. Harney of the chamber of commerce, and Leon Block, a friend of Rogers'. Gurkin presented her with a Norfolk commemorative half dollar, a book on Norfolk, and a card giving her the courtesies of the city. The key Miss Pickford is holding in her hand was not given to her by Mayor Gurkin; it was given by Mayor Bright of Richmond when she stopped there enroute to Norfolk.

It developed that Rogers had a near-attack of pneumonia, but quickly recovered. Miss Pickford went on to South Boston, where she was crowned the following Tuesday, after which she returned to Norfolk, met her husband, and flew to New York in his private plane. Photographs by Charles Borges, Virginian-Pilot; courtesy of John A. Gurkin, Jr.

A common scene in years gone by on the Norfolk-Portsmouth waterfront was the shuttling of freight barges of railroads operating in the area to and from their various terminals. This scene, about 1939, shows the Norfolk Southern railroad tug Lynnhaven conveying a house barge loaded with freight from its slip on Water Street (now referred to as Dunmore Docks) to the railroad's terminal in Berkley. The ferry to the right is the Norfolk County Number 2, operating between Norfolk and Portsmouth. Ferry service ceased in 1954. Photograph by H. D. Vollmer

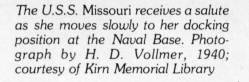

The U.S.S. Missouri receives a salute as she moves slowly to her docking position at the Naval Base. Photograph by H. D. Vollmer, 1940; courtesy of Kirn Memorial Library

City Hall Avenue from the Royster Building during the beginning of a northeast gale in 1938. Once a creek extending almost to Church Street (St. Paul Boulevard) the street has been filled in over the years; however, it is lower than the rest of the area, causing it to flood quickly, often impassable for pedestrians and vehicles. Flood walls and gates on Boush Street were built during the 1960s to prevent flooding. Photographs by Carroll Walker

Looking north from the west side of Granby Street and Market Street in 1941. Courtesy of Kirn Memorial Library

This nighttime scene shows Granby Street between Market and Freemason streets during the summer of 1941. Parking was allowed on both sides of the street at that time, and many people would drive downtown and park on the street just to watch the crowds pass by. Courtesy of Kirn Memorial Library

Fire destroyed the grain elevator of the Norfolk and Western Railroad at its Norfolk Yard at the foot of East Main Street on September 24, 1941. The elevator, a six-story structure, was erected in 1887, and for more than half a century it was a landmark for the train passengers coming into Norfolk over the Norfolk and Western Railway. The elevator was a total loss and never rebuilt. Photograph by Charles J. Borjes

In this 1960 view Janaf Shopping Center had been built on the site of Glen Rock Airport. On the left in the airport picture is a slanting dark line, a drainage ditch, which runs behind the airport buildings. The ditch still exists, running parallel with the road just left of the parking area. A section of the Virginia Beach Boulevard shows in the lower left. Courtesy of Kirn Memorial Library

One of Norfolk's earliest flying fields was the Glen Rock Airport, which came into existence in the early '30s. It was located on the present site of the Janaf Shopping Center. At that time the area was farmland in Norfolk County. The airport consisted of two buildings, one of which was a new administration building. Small planes, such as Piper Cubs, used the field, which was grassy and shaped somewhat like a golf course dog leg. The highway is the three-lane Virginia Beach Boulevard.

Many famous flyers, such as "Wrong Way" Corrigan and Wiley Post, used the field. Demonstrations, stunt flying, student instruction, and charter flights were regular activities. Many Norfolkians learned to fly on this field. This picture was taken by J. V. Croom in 1941 from a Piper Cub. He used a box camera.

Captain Lord Louis Mountbatten, Royal Navy, inspects British marines on board the carrier H. M. S. Illustrious as he takes command of the ship at the Norfolk Navy Yard. The Illustrious and a companion carrier, the Formidable, were severely mauled by German planes while on duty in the Mediterranean during the summer of 1941. They were of necessity sent secretly to Norfolk for repairs. Photograph by H. D. Vollmer, Norfolk Ledger-Dispatch.

In 1942 the Norfolk Theatre Managers Association got together to plan a campaign to sell U.S. War Savings Stamps and Bonds. In the picture are, left to right: Langhorne Weiford, Kopeland Ornoff, Sydney Gates (ex-president and sandwiched in between signs), president Jeff Hofheimer, R. R. Drissel, Pierre Boulogne, Stanley Barr, George R. Loeffert, and Melzer Diggs. Photograph by Charles Borjes; courtesy of Beverley B. Hainer

When the Nansemond Hotel was built at Ocean View in 1928 the Spanish-style architecture and the dining room and ballroom overlooking the Chesapeake Bay led to its immediate popularity with Tidewater residents and out-of-town visitors.

The resort gained strategic importance when the United States entered World War II and the Nansemond was selected as headquarters for amphibious operations. It was ideally situated with its beachfront on the bay where landing craft could be beached and with its proximity to the Naval Base, to Little Creek, and to the ferry landing at Willoughby Spit. On August 15, 1942, the hotel became official headquarters of the Commander, Amphibious Force, U.S. Atlantic Fleet, and remained so until August 15, 1945. Every inch of the hotel was under military command. Here the invasion of North Africa would be conceived and designated as "Torch." On October 24, 1945, a fleet of 107 vessels left Hampton Roads for North Africa. The rest is history.

The hotel is shown in 1945; the lobby view is from 1935. Courtesy of Norfolk Historical Society

After the hotel was returned to its owners on August 15, 1945, it began a slow decline. Plans to upgrade it did not materialize. When the end came, it was complete and swift. On the night of November 21, 1980, the Nansemond was totally destroyed by fire.

Nothing remained the following morning except a few smoking walls—and the memories of those who had enjoyed its hospitality and conviviality during brighter days.

The remains of the Nansemond Hotel after the destructive fire bore a strange resemblance to scenes in North Africa, inadvertently created by the planning at the hotel for the North African invasion. Photograph by Carroll Walker

Bob Rowe and Dean Atkinson lead in their Hampton One design in the Maury Regatta of 1947 off the entrance to the Lafayette River. The Hampton Boulevard Bridge can be seen in the background. Photograph by H. D. Vollmer

In 1948 the government of Generalissimo Chiang Kai-shek acquired some small naval vessels from the United States for use by the Chinese navy. Officers and other personnel were sent to the United States to familiarize themselves with the use of such craft. Several hundred came to Norfolk.

Taken in the auditorium of the old Chinese Merchants Association on Church Street, this photograph shows some of the men who were stationed temporarily at the Navy Yard and who returned shortly afterwards to China. The late Leon Nowitzky, Norfolk's chief of detectives for many years, sits in the front row with a small Chinese boy. Photograph by Carroll Walker

Many people who traveled back and forth on Monticello Avenue hardly noticed the convent that stood in the 700 block of Monticello Avenue. This was the Convent of the Franciscan Sisters in charge of Our Lady and St. Francis, established in the early part of this century to furnish the teachers for St. Joseph's Catholic School on East Queen Street. It was demolished in the early 1950s when the area was cleared for the first phase of Norfolk's downtown redevelopment. The picture was taken in 1949. *Courtesy of Kirn Memorial Library*

This aerial view of the heart of downtown Norfolk was taken in 1950. In the upper right the city's gas works are seen. Below in the center left is the Monticello Hotel. In the center is the National Bank of Commerce Building, later to become the First and Mer-chants National Bank when the Virginia National Bank is built at the top of Commercial Place (bottom center). At one time the slip at Roanoke Avenue (just left of the ferry) extended halfway to water Street. Known as Roanoke Dock, it was the center of Norfolk's produce business. One ferry is in its slip in this view; in a few years the ferries would cease to run when the new Norfolk-Portsmouth Tunnel began operating *Courtesy of Kirn Memorial Library*

This is the tip end of Willoughby Spit in 1950. It is the general opinion that Willoughby Spit came into existence in 1749 during a hurricane, although some sources claim it may have happened later. The area gets its name from Capt. Thomas Willoughby, who came to Virginia in 1619. In 1626 he owned a large tract of land in the Ocean View area. Courtesy of Elizabeth G. Gresham

In 1951 the city of Norfolk began the conversion of some of its slum areas into housing units for the people living there. These pictures show some of the conditions existing in the area between Brambleton Avenue and Princess Anne Road and Monticello Avenue on the west. Many of the streets in this area were shortened or lost their identity completely. This unit was to be called Young Park. It was ready by 1953 when people started moving in. Courtesy of Norfolk Redevelopment and Housing Authority

New housing in another converted slum area facing Tidewater Drive. Known as Tidewater Park, it was begun in 1953 and ready for tenants in 1955. Courtesy of Norfolk Redevelopment and Housing Authority

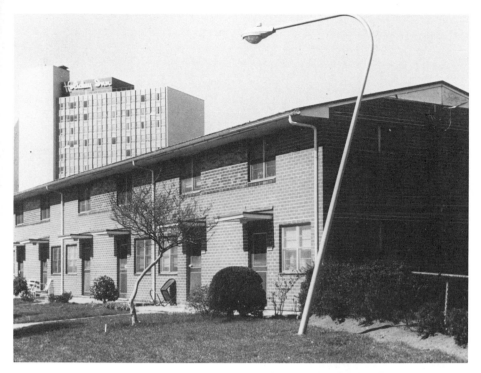

These are pictures of Young Park just off Monticello and Brambleton Avenues, the first phase of Norfolk's slum conversion program. It was begun in 1951, and the first families moved in 1953. Courtesy of Norfolk Redevelopment and Housing Authority

In the dark days of slavery, two slave women, Annette M. Lane of Norfolk and Harriet R. Taylor of Hampton, aided by two abolitionists, Joshua R. Giddings and Joliffe Union, operating in strict secrecy, set up an underground railway for slaves in this area. In 1867, two years after the War Between the States was over, the organization shed its secrecy and was formally organized in Norfolk as the United Order of Tents, J. R. G., and J. U., incorporating in its name the initials of the two abolitionists who originally aided them. With its aims basically charitable work, it maintains a home for the elderly in Hampton. The organization is considered one of the most important women's lodges in the United States. The building in this picture was constructed in 1913. It was replaced by another building in 1961 and is located at 1620 Church Street. Courtesy of Kirn Memorial Library

These fishing trawlers are tied up at the old Pennsylvania Railroad pier-warehouse at the end of Brooke Avenue. Mostly out of New England, they usually came south during the winter months because southern waters were less hazardous. Often when the weather became too stormy off the Virginia coast or when the boats were in need of provisions, they came into Norfolk. The old pier-warehouse has been demolished, and the boats are less frequently seen in Norfolk. Photograph by H. D. Vollmer, 1953

An ice-encrusted trawler comes in from the sea and docks at the Boush Cold Storage pier at the foot of City Hall Avenue. Photograph by Charles J. Borjes, 1950

The steamer United States passes the piers and warehouses of the Old Bay Line Steamship Company and the Merchants and Miners Transportation Company at the foot of West Main Street (Towne Point) in November 1954. The vessel has just left the Navy Yard after repairs; it would make a similar trip in July 1980. Photograph by Perry Breon

The tanker Chevron Eindnoven passes Towne Point at the foot of West Main Street in July 1979. It is interesting to compare the changes in Norfolk's waterfront since the United States passed the same area in 1954. Courtesy of Norfolk Newspapers

On July 1, 1909, the first passenger train over the newly built Virginian Railway arrived in Norfolk. On January 29, 1956—and pictured here—the last Virginian passenger train Number 3, still using steam locomotives, left Norfolk on its final run for Roanoke, Virginia. The old Union Station, completed in 1912, is shown in the background. It was taken down in 1963. While the Virginian Railway handled passengers and general freight from its western terminus at Deepwater, West Virginia, its main commodity was coal. On December 31, 1959, the company ceased to exist when it became a part of the Norfolk and Western Railway system. Photograph by H. D. Vollmer

Granby Street from Freemason Street looking south at night, circa 1950. Photograph by H. D. Vollmer

A daytime view of Granby from Freemason, circa 1952. Photograph by H. D. Vollmer

The same view in 1980. Photograph by Carroll Walker

The Susan Constant, *a replica of one of the three ships that brought Virginia's first settlers from England in 1607, sails upon Hampton Roads off Fort Wool in 1957 on the 350th anniversary of the founding of the first* English settlement at Jamestown. *This ship, together with replicas of the other two ships that accompanied her, the* Godspeed *and* Discovery, *are now docked at Jamestown. Courtesy of Norfolk Historical Society*

This beautiful house on the corner of Freemason and Dunmore streets was built sometime before the turn of the century and was the home of Minton W. Talbot, whose forebears settled in the Norfolk area long before 1700. The picture was taken in 1940, and the house was taken down in the 1950s. Courtesy of Kirn Memorial Library

The Tadlock brothers were professional racers. John, the oldest, began racing ponies at age eleven, and at fifteen (claiming he was twenty-one), he drove a four-cylinder Essex at the Widgeon track located west of Bay View Boulevard and Granby Street. It was his first auto race, and he won. In 1928 he was joined by his brother Eldridge and in 1930 by brother Monk. They raced all over the country.

In 1932 John was injured in an accident and forced to participate only from the "pits," but he became an expert mechanic. When Eldridge was killed in an automobile accident in 1942, John sold his racing equipment and concentrated on repairing and later building automobiles. In 1955 well-known racer Jack Weatherly drove five racers for Tadlock and won them all.

In one instance a millionaire who was a racing enthusiast flew to Norfolk to buy one of John Tadlock's cars. When it needed repairs in 1957, he had Tadlock flown to Key West to make them.

In 1981 John Tadlock is still tinkering with cars.

This 1929 photograph shows John Tadlock in his Model A Ford racing car at Newport News Fair Grounds, where he won three out of five races. Courtesy of John Tadlock

John Tadlock became interested in midget car racing, which was popular in the middle 1940s. In 1945 Tadlock was awarded a trophy for one of his midgets, Number 8, setting a record at Daytona Beach on a mile straightaway. His car was powered by an Offenhauser engine, one of the best in the field. This is one of his midgets in 1947. Courtesy of John Tadlock

John Tadlock (center) receives the trophy for setting a record at Daytona Beach, Florida, in 1954. Steve McCarthy, driver of the car, is on the left, and Pat Purcell from Daytona on the right. Courtesy of John Tadlock

For years the Norfolk Chamber of Commerce has held a summer outing for the benefit of its members and their friends. The two men in this picture, namely, the late Alex Bell, City Treasurer for many years, and Dr. Southgate Leigh, Jr., both members of the chamber at the time this picture was taken in 1954, prepare to sample some of the good doctor's concoction of "herbal medicine," consisting of choice mint leaves, maybe a pinch or two of powdered sugar, and a liberal addition of "Oh Bee Joyfull," which produced a quality mint julep and which enhanced the doctor's reputation. Whether or not they had anything to do with the Health and Sanitation Committee is not known, but obviously they were in a good position to sanitize anything if so required. Courtesy Southgate Lee III

An aerial view of Ghent on the center right and a part of Atlantic City on the bottom in 1959. Circular Mowbray Arch fronts the Hague, which is crossed by the Ghent Bridge in the center. In the lower right is the Atlantic City Bridge. Courtesy of Kirn Memorial Library

Modern Life

1960~1980

This view shows a part of Commercial Place and East Main Street looking east in 1960. The Confederate Monument is still in its original position at the head of Commercial Place in front of the W. G. Swartz Company department store. With the exception of the monument, all other buildings have since disappeared. The building in the upper left is the new city jail under construction. Photograph by Carroll Walker

Commercial Place and East Main in 1980. The Virginia National Bank parking ramp is on the left, and above it is a portion of the United Virginia Bank. A section of the city jail is visible in the upper left. The building in the upper center is the First Virginia Bank Tower on St. Paul Boulevard and Waterfront Drive. The entrance to the Royster Building is on the center left and the Virginia National Bank Building is located behind the hedging in the lower right. Before construction began on the Virginia National Bank Building, the Confederate Monument was taken down temporarily and stored because it might sustain damage if too close to the construction work. A few years after the bank building was completed in 1967, the monument was replaced, this time about 150 feet northeast of its former position. Photograph by Carroll Walker

In 1960 the corner of Olney Road and Mowbray Arch by the Chrysler Museum looked like this. At one time much of this area was a part of Smith Creek, which extended almost to Church Street. Even after the creek was filled in and the streets paved, the area flooded during storms, making some of the streets impassable. The apartment building in the center was located on Hamilton Avenue, which street disappeared along with several others, such as Ward Avenue, Duncan Avenue, and parts of Duke Street and Omohundro and Moran avenues. Note from the sign on the left that gasoline cost as little as 21.9¢ per gallon in 1960. Photograph by Carroll Walker

Olney Road and Mowbray Arch in 1980. Buildings had been torn down; some streets had been eliminated and new ones created. Many new homes had already been built and more were under construction when this picture was taken. Photograph by Carroll Walker

This view of the old Atlantic City Bridge was taken in 1960 from Mowbray Arch in Ghent before it was replaced by a new bridge in 1963. Photograph by Carroll Walker

Originated in 1961 as the Norfolk Civic Ballet Company with Gene Hammett as artistic director, this talented company has become the Tidewater Ballet Association. Hammett remains artistic director and Polly Martin is executive administrator.

Former students have become permanent members of several prestigious ballet companies and have been top candidates for major dance scholarships. One TBA student startled the dance world with her magnificent performance in Swan Lake, May 1981 in Towson, Maryland. Seventeen-year-old Christie Herrin became a last-minute replacement for Gelsey Kirkland of Baryshnikov's American Ballet Theatre, dancing with Patrick Bissell, ABT's lead male dancer, to wide acclaim.

This photograph shows the Tidewater Ballet Association in Swan Lake. Courtesy of Gene Hammett

A new Norfolk begins to rise as the old awaits destruction. At East Main and Church streets in 1961, the new city jail and courthouse in the center—the first phase of redevelopment of downtown Norfolk—have just been completed. The old buildings in the foreground, which housed beer taverns of all descriptions extending to Commercial Place, will come down soon. The gray building partially shown in the center right was originally French's Tavern. By an odd coincidence, the day the hotel opened April 17, 1837, Prince Louis Napoleon Bonaparte, later Emperor Napoleon III of France, was visiting Norfolk with his entourage. Let it suffice to say the occasion was royally observed at the hotel. Photograph by Carroll Walker

A part of East Main Street extending from the Confederate Monument to the Union Station once was a sleazy, honky tonk area, filled with beer taverns of all descriptions. When the city embarked upon its program of the redevelopment of the downtown area in 1959, the end of this area was in sight. However, rather than wait for the bulldozers to wreak havoc on the taverns, fire broke out in one of them on the night of February 2, 1961, bringing about the premature destruction of a number of buildings. One of the most popular taverns was The Shamrock, shown in this picture, always conspicuous by the revolving barrel over the entrance. Photograph by Carroll Walker, 1961

191

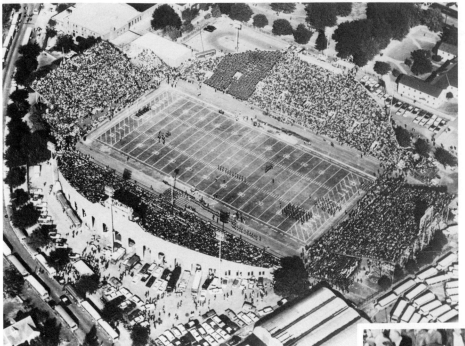

The Navy-Pitt Game at the Oyster Bowl, 1962. Each year the Shrine-Khedive Temple of Norfolk sponsors a football classic of two well-known teams. The game, known as the Oyster Bowl, takes place in the stadium of Old Dominion University. With the exception of one year, this game has been given every year since 1947, and it is always a sell-out, with proceeds going to a hospital for crippled children. In the inset picture are Judge Walter E. Hoffman, M. T. Blassingham, Sr. (the "Father of the Oyster Bowl"), Herman S. Nowitsky, and Aubrey G. Graham, all past potentates of Khedive Temple. Graham was Imperial Potentate of the Shrine of North America in 1970. Courtesy of Khedive Temple

Aerial view of the merchandise piers of the Norfolk and Western Railway at Lambert's Point. Above the piers can be seen the storage tracks holding hundreds of cars of coal for transshipment to foreign countries. Photograph by E. E. Vickhouse, 1965

President and Mrs. Lyndon Johnson attend the coronation of their daughter, Luci Baines, at the 1965 Azalea Festival, where she became Queen Azalea XII. On the left of the President is Lynda Bird Johnson, who had been crowned Queen Azalea VI in 1961 and who now lives in Virginia with her husband Charles Robb. Courtesy of Kirn Memorial Library

Brambleton Avenue came into existence after the development of Brambleton began in the 1870s. Its western termination was at a finger of Newton's Creek west of Maltby Avenue. This end of the creek extended northward across what is now Princess Anne Road. Queen Street was on the opposite side of the creek, in existence since before 1800, and ran westward across town to Boush Street.

When a part of George Bramble's farm was sold in 1870, a causeway was constructed over the remainder of this part of the creek. It was slowly being filled in and connected with what was to become Brambleton Avenue. Now for the first time Norfolk could be entered from the east instead of the old Church Street route. The suburb grew rapidly and was annexed by Norfolk in 1877. The Queen Street-Brambleton Avenue route became an important east-west thoroughfare.

After the massive annexation of Norfolk's outlying areas in 1923, the city undertook the task of revising the names of streets in Norfolk. It was decided to extend Brambleton Avenue to Boush Street and to eliminate Queen Street.

In the redevelopment of the downtown area in the 1950s and in order to expedite the east-west flow of traffic across town, Brambleton Avenue was extended west to connect with Hampton Boulevard at Redgate Avenue in Ghent. The work started around 1960, the date of this picture taken by Eugene G. Vickhouse.

Construction of the extension is under way in this view, taken February 12, 1962, by William Abourjille.

February 24, 1964: the Brambleton Avenue extension is complete. Courtesy of Norfolk Historical Society

The fourth picture, taken by Carroll Walker in January 1981, shows Brambleton Avenue as it appears now. The YMCA building in the center left is more visible, as are the Botetourt Apartments. The tall building on the left is the Hague Apartments, built in 1965 and the high rise at right is Hague Towers. This entire series was photographed from atop the Virginian Pilot and Ledger-Star buildings.

An aerial view taken about 1967 shows Norfolk's rapidly expanding Medical Center on Colley and Brambleton avenues. The Norfolk General Hospital is in the center; to the left are older buildings and quarters for nursing and other personnel. Another addition is now being made to the hospital. The Medical Tower is in the center right. Snaking around the complex from the top center is Brambleton Avenue, which connects with Hampton Boulevard on the left. In the upper left is the Ghent residential section. *Courtesy of Norfolk Chamber of Commerce*

In 1967 the Norfolk Museum of Arts and Sciences (now the Chrysler Museum), in an effort to raise funds for the museum, turned the old Ghent Bridge into their own version of the Ponte Vecchio. Like its namesake in Florence, Italy, it featured stalls and booths on both sides of the bridge, dispensing food and drink to the crowds as well as selling various mementos. *Photograph by Frank Dill*

In 1934 George Brown, an insurance salesman, aware of the lack of college opportunities for Negroes, was able to secure for Norfolk a two-year branch of the Virginia Union University with the help of a few others.

With no building available, they rented two rooms in a building that belonged to a fraternal club on Brambleton Avenue. One room was used as an office and library and the other was a classroom. Several teachers came down from Richmond during the week to teach math, English, science, and sociology; eighty-five students were enrolled the first year.

The college grew and on February 1, 1968, it severed its connection with the Virginia Union University and became independent, becoming known as Norfolk State College. Since that time the school has greatly expanded, adding two large dormitories on Park Avenue. A few years ago it became Norfolk State University. It now has an enrollment of approximately 7,000 students. Photograph by Carroll Walker

The Administration Building and a part of the flying field of Norfolk Airport as it appeared in 1968. Since then the size of the field has been increased and a new administration building erected to the right of the cars in this picture. This airport was built in 1939. Prior to that time it had been a golf course. Photograph by S. H. Ringo

In 1969 work began on a new enclosed shopping center on Military Highway between, in general, the old Virginia Beach Boulevard on the west and the Virginia Beach Expressway on the east. It was to be known as the Military Circle. This picture was taken in February 1969, after work had begun on the project. Three of the main buildings are under construction. Courtesy of Military Circle Shopping Center

In ten years time the Military Circle Shopping Center has greatly expanded, as this picture shows. Within the circle the square building on the left is Thalheimer's, in the upper left center Miller and Rhoads, on the far right Leggett's, and in the bottom center the J. C. Penney Company. All are well known department stores. This picture was taken in December 1980. Courtesy of Military Circle Shopping Center

A new park known as MacArthur Square has been created in downtown Norfolk at City Hall Avenue, Plume, and Bank streets. The main attraction is the old courthouse on the right, built in 1850, but converted in 1960 to the MacArthur Memorial in which General MacArthur is interred. A small museum and theatre are located in the square. The buildings in the background of this 1979 picture are, left to right: the tall white Royster Building behind the Kirn Memorial Library, the new Federal Building behind the Rennert Garage, and the Maritime Tower. Photograph by Carroll Walker

His Excellency, the ambassador from Japan to the United States, Nobuhiko Ushiba (center) admires a medal presented to him by W. Fred Duckworth (left), president of the MacArthur Memorial Foundation, during the ambassador's visit to the memorial in 1971. Mayor Roy B. Martin, Jr., looks on. Courtesy of Chamber of Commerce

In September 1911, the John T. West School introduced high school level subjects for blacks in Norfolk, and in June 1915 its first graduates were awarded diplomas.

A football team was organized in 1914, presumably the first black high school football team in the city. The team was financed by the sale of season tickets, and each member had to buy his own uniform.

In December 1916 the city school board purchased the Norfolk Mission College on the corner of Princess Anne Road and Charles Street and moved the West High School department to this building, renaming it the Booker T. Washington High School. A football team was also organized at the school, playing its first game in 1917. The Norfolk Mission College is shown in the inset.

As the pupils increased, a new high school building was constructed in 1922 on Princess Anne Road, classes beginning there in January 1922. Its first principal was Charles W. Reynolds. As the building outlived its usefulness and became overcrowded, a site was selected for a new high school on the corner of East Princess Anne Road and Park Avenue. The modern building with a capacity for 2,000 students, opened in 1974. Photograph by Carroll Walker

For many years it was felt that Norfolk was an ideal place for the location of a medical school. The Eastern Virginia Medical School opened in September 1973, one of the most modern of its kind. It is located on the corner of Colley Avenue and Olney Road. At the present time there are 280 students enrolled in the school. Photograph by Carroll Walker, 1981

An aerial view of Scope and the Chrysler Theatre area taken in 1975. Monticello Avenue runs from the center left to meet with St. Paul Boulevard in the upper right, both crossing Brambleton Avenue. Photograph by S. H. Ringo

In 1974 a group of opera lovers got together to bring opera to Norfolk, and out of this meeting came the Virginia Opera Association. Edythe Harrison became its first president.

In 1975 Peter Mark was appointed artistic director for the opera company. His wife, Thea Musgrave, a distinguished composer, joined him in Norfolk and began to compose Mary, Queen of Scots, a new opera. In the summer of 1977 Thea Musgrave's Mary, Queen of Scots premiered at the Edinburgh Festival in Scotland, where it was warmly received. Its United States premier was held in Norfolk in 1978.

In 1978 Musgrave was commissioned by the Virginia Opera Association to compose an opera for Christmas, which resulted in an adaptation of Charles Dickens' A Christmas Carol. It made its premiere at the Center Theatre on December 4, 1979, and is pictured here.

Although only six years old, The Virginia Opera Association has made an outstanding name for itself in the musical world.

The first train of the Norfolk and Western Railway (then the Norfolk and Petersburg Railroad) came into Norfolk at the foot of East Main Street in 1859. The railroad expanded its operations after the War Between the States, building a coal pier in the Lambert's Point section of Norfolk. The first coal train for this new pier arrived in 1883. Since that time other piers have been built and replaced. This picture, taken in 1975, shows two colliers taking on coal at Pier Number 6, built in 1962. A portion of the railroad's vast storage yard, capable of handling over 7,000 cars, is shown here. The company's merchandise piers are shown in the upper center of the picture. Photograph by E. G. Vickhouse

John Burton (left), glad-hand-wringer for the Hospitality Committee of the Norfolk Chamber of Commerce, welcomes underwater sea explorer Jacques Cousteau to Norfolk on his visit here in 1979. Since his visit here, the Cousteau Society has moved its headquarters to a building on Twenty-First Street, and Cousteau's research vessel Calypso has become a regular feature of the Norfolk waterfront. At one time John Burton and Kopeland Ornoff were designated as Norfolk's "Ambassadors at Large." Photograph by Carroll Walker

201

Visitors to the Ocean View Amusement Park fifty or sixty years ago soon became aware of a tantalizing aroma in the air, and it didn't take long to discover that its origin was the Doumar ice cream stand. Soon you were one of the throng munching on a delicious handmade, waffle-like ice cream cone filled with ice cream.

This stand was operated by George Doumar, whose brother Abe was credited with introducing the ice cream cone to the world at the St. Louis Exposition in 1904. Not long from Lebanon, Abe met a concessionaire at the fair who was selling waffles at one cent apiece next to an ice cream stand. Abe suggested making a cone out of a waffle, filling it with ice cream, calling it a cornucopia, and selling it for ten cents. Dubious at first, the waffle seller let Abe have a fling at it—and the ice cream cone was born.

When the exposition was over, the concessionaire gave Abe one of his waffle irons. After Abe returned to his home in New Jersey, he developed a four-iron baking machine from it, fired by charcoal and later by butane gas. A foundry nearby made the machines for him, which he not only used himself, but sold to others. However, he kept the molds bearing his name.

In 1905 Abe Doumar put his machines to work at a stand in Coney Island. This venture was not too successful at first, but when he hired some attractive girls to stroll around the place eating ice cream cones, sales picked up. In the meantime, George Doumar and two other brothers arrived from Lebanon and were put to work at stands in other locations, George and Coney Island.

Abe had planned to operate a stand at the Jamestown Exposition in 1907 but lost out when someone else got there ahead of him. Instead, he moved to the Ocean View Amusement Park where he was quite successful. Abe liked the resort, and he moved his family from New Jersey to Norfolk. His brother George soon joined him and operated the stand at Ocean View. At a picnic for the employees of the Virginia Railway and Power Company at Ocean View, George sold a record 22,600 cones.

Abe died in 1947, but George

Doumar continued the operations at Ocean View until the great hurricane of August 23, 1933, when much of the amusement park was destroyed. In 1934 he opened the present drive-in on Monticello Avenue between Nineteenth and Twentieth streets, which has been improved and enlarged over the years. George passed away in 1970, and the place is run by his sons, Al and Vic.

On July 21, 1979, Vic and Al Doumar observed the seventy-fifth birthday of Doumar's by offering all ice cream cones that day for ten cents each. To the delight of their customers, they brought out their seventy-five-year-old waffle machine, with which they still make their cones, and let their customers watch them make the famous "Doumar" cone—just as Abe did seventy-five years before.

George Doumar serves an ice cream cone while his sons, Al, John, and Vic look on. Courtesy of Al and Vic Doumar

Known first as the German Naval sail training ship Horst Wessel, built in 1936 in Hamburg, Germany, this ship was claimed by the United States in 1946 as a war reparation. She was renamed the Eagle, after a long line of famous U.S. revenue cutters. The Eagle often makes an annual cruise to European waters with the Coast Guard Academy's 1st and 3rd classes aboard. Later, on a shorter cruise, she takes the 2nd and 4th classes aboard. Wherever she goes, she attracts large crowds, and her frequent visits do much to publicize the work done by the U.S. Coast Guard. This picture was taken in 1974. Courtesy of Kirn Memorial Library

The full-rigged Norwegian training ship Christian Radich visited Norfolk in 1975. It was built in 1937 and has an overall length of 238 feet. She was visiting the New York World's Fair in 1939 when World War II began. She sailed home, joined the Norwegian fleet, was seized by Germans in 1940 and used as a depot ship. She was sunk and raised after the war. Photograph by Carroll Walker

The full-rigged Danish training ship Danmark has visited Norfolk a number of times. She was built in 1932 and has an overall length of 252 feet. Like the Christian Radich, she was visiting the New York World's Fair in 1939 when World War II broke out. She was loaned to the U.S. Coast Guard for the duration, for training. She returned home in 1959 and carries a plaque expressing America's thanks. The Danmark was in Norfolk in 1976 for "Operation Sail." Photograph by Carroll Walker

In 1977 the Norfolk School of Boatbuilding was established to revive the art of wooden boatbuilding and to train young men and women to enter maritime trades. The program includes basic naval architecture and ship design, woodworking techniques, lofting, spar making, sail making, rigging, outfitting and small boat handling. Located in the old C&O warehouse-pier at the foot of Brooke Avenue in the Southgate Terminal, the school has become well known along the coast and has attracted visits from sailing craft of all designs, particularly during the annual Harborfest. Photograph by Carroll Walker

Joseph A. Filipowski, director of promotions at the Norfolk School of Boatbuilding, adds a finishing touch to the Swan. Photograph by Carroll Walker

Temple Ohef Sholom and the Ghent Methodist Church share two opposite corners on Raleigh Avenue and Stockley Gardens. The synagogue was erected in 1918 after its temple on Monticello Avenue and Freemason Street was destroyed by fire. The Ghent Methodist Society was organized in 1902, building a temporary tabernacle later that year. In 1921 the present church was constructed, modeled after London's St. Martin's-in-the-Field. Photograph by Carroll Walker, 1977

A wild and turbulent sky swirls over downtown Norfolk as an autumnal storm abates. Taken from East Bute Street near St. Paul Boulevard, the picture covers an area from the Rotunda Building (left) on St. Paul Boulevard to the Freemason Street Baptist Church on the right. In the sweep of the picture are Plaza One, Bank of Virginia, United Virginia Bank, old Norfolk Academy (now Chamber of Commerce), Virginia National Bank (partially hidden by tree). The automobiles are on St. Paul Boulevard. Photograph by Carroll Walker, 1980

At the confluence of the Eastern and Southern branches of the Elizabeth River is the Norfolk Shipbuilding & Drydock Corporation, now known as Norshipco (center), the newest part of which is located on the old Norfolk Southern Railroad terminal in the Berkley section of Norfolk.

Norshipco was organized in 1917 and ultimately operated in both Norfolk and Berkley as it expanded. In 1970 the company acquired the Norfolk Southern property of about twenty acres, which adjoined their Berkley plant, and erected on it one of the nation's largest floating drydocks and a 1,030-foot pier next to it. This activity is shown in the eye-level picture. One ship is in the floating drydock and the other is tied up alongside the pier. The steamer United States was recently checked over in this dry dock in 1980 when a possible sale was thought imminent for it. In the distance on the right are the grain elevators of the Carghill Grain Company and the large crane of the Navy Yard in Portsmouth.

The plant in this aerial view is contained more or less within the triangle formed by the two roads coming to an apex in the center of the picture and the river. The huge drydock is located in the center left, the larger boat being in the drydock, while the smaller boat is tied up at the 1,030-foot pier. Photograph by Jim Backus

A daytime view of the steamer United States *in Norshipco's drydock. The tanker is tied up at a pier. Photograph by Jim Backus*

The steamer United States *in dry dock at the Norshipco plant in Berkley at night. Original photograph in color by Tal Carey*

In the fall of 1977 Marianne C. Stanley became women's basketball coach at Old Dominion University. In three years she turned the Lady Monarchs into the most outstanding women's basketball team in the country: National Women's Invitational Tournament Champions in 1977-78; AIAW National Champions in 1978-79 and 1979-80.

Among the outstanding players were Inge Nissen, a 6'5" center, and 5'9" Nancy Lieberman. By the end of her senior year Nissen had become the university's all-time leading scorer for women's basketball with 2,647 points and an all-time rebounder with 1,509 points. Lieberman was regarded as a razzle-dazzle player who put zip into the game. In four years she earned more honors than any other athlete had ever achieved, including three-time All-American and winner of two consecutive Wade trophies and Broderick awards.

On June 16, 1980, the Women's Professional Basketball League

drafted eight players from the 1979-80 Lady Monarchs team, including all seven players and one returning player—the first time in any draft that so many players from a single team would be selected.

Pictured are the award-winning Lady Monarchs of 1978-79. Left to right, standing: Coach Marianne C. Stanley, Nancy Lieberman, Jan Trombley, Susan Richardson, Inge Nissen, Linda Jerome, Chris Critelli, Rhonda Rompola, Angela Cotman, assistant coach Jerry Busone. Kneeling: Sue Brown, Sandy Burke, Debbie Richard, Sue Davy, Beth Campbell, and Fran Clemente. Courtesy of Old Dominion University

The First Baptist Church, 418 East Bute Street, is one of Norfolk's most attractive and interesting churches. It was organized in 1800 as an interracial church and worshipped in the Borough Church known as St. Paul's Episcopal. By 1815 its total membership was 278. A separation took place in 1816 when some members of the church withdrew to found a new organization, and this group was known for many years as the Cumberland Street Baptists. In 1830 the Bute Street site was purchased, where the congregation worshipped in a building known as the "Old Salt Box." In 1859 a new church building was dedicated. In 1876 the church burned down and a new one was rebuilt in 1877. In 1906 the present building of stone and brick was built. Photograph by Carroll Walker, 1980

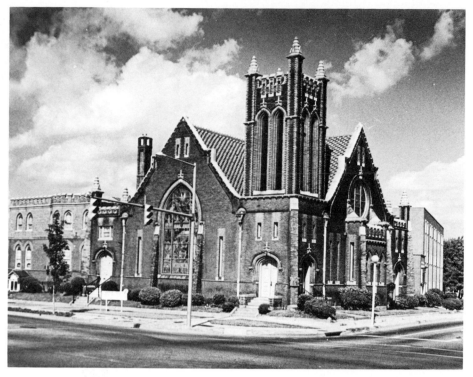

For years the attractiveness of the Central Baptist Church on the corner of Manteo Street and West Olney Road in Ghent went virtually unnoticed until the trees surrounding it were cut down and the streets widened, giving the building more "breathing space." The church was built about 1905. Photograph by Carroll Walker, 1980

This Gothic structure is the St. John African Methodist Episcopal Church, 545 East Bute Street, and the Mother Church of African Methodism in Virginia. It was originally conceived as a mission for Negro slaves within the Cumberland Street Methodist Church in 1840. Rapid growth required larger quarters, resulting in the congregation moving into an old soap factory. In 1848 the present church site was acquired and a small building erected. In 1863 the congregation petitioned the Baltimore Conference of the African Methodist Episcopal Church for acceptance. Started in 1787 in Philadelphia by Negroes who left St. George, the first Methodist Church in America, the denomination was organized officially in Baltimore in 1816. St. John was received into the A.M.E. Connection on January 1, 1864. In 1868 the first church was rebuilt and enlarged, and in 1888 the present structure was constructed by members from the ground up. Photograph by Carroll Walker, 1980

Sometime after the Iranian government seized the American Embassy in Teheran and made its occupants hostages, the Dominion National Bank on City Hall Avenue and Monticello Avenue flew from its building a large flag showing on it "Free the Hostages" on a yellow background. When the hostages were finally released on January 12, 1981, the bank withdrew the flag and replaced it with another, expressing on it the sentiments of the nation—"Hallelujah." Photograph by Carroll Walker

Norfolk: A Pictorial History (1975) offered pictures of a restaurant on East Main Street near Commerce Street known as Steinhilber's or "Steiney's." It was run by Walter Steinhilber for almost fifty years, and a host of his friends from local businesses and politics patronized it. When the downtown renewal program began in the 1960s and various businesses began to disappear, so did his customers, which saddened Steinhilber. In 1967 he passed away. If ever a person passed away at the right time, he did—as his world came tumbling down.

Across the street from Steiney's is the Snug Harbor restaurant in the Selden Arcade, built on the site of the old Academy of Music. Robert "Bob" Fitzgerald, operator of Snug Harbor, offered to provide a special table for the "Steinhilber Alumni," many of whom can be seen there at

midday chasing the festive mutton chop, laughing, reminiscing, or settling the world's problems.

Here R. K. T. "Kit" Larsen, Ver-

non Hitchings, Charles Drescher, and Robert Summers meet at the Snug Harbor. Photograph by Carroll Walker

Bob Fitzgerald greets patrons of the "Steiney's Alumni" table at Snug Harbor. Photograph by Carroll Walker

Lou Hertz does a ballet with a coffeepot at Snug Harbor. Photograph by Carroll Walker

Left to right: Sam Ames, Ted Pilcher, and Bill Ames. Photograph by Carroll Walker

Left to right: Ray Robinson, A. J. "Preacher" Parsons, and Sam Ames.

The Khedive Highlanders' Band of Norfolk, wearing the tartan of the Buchanan Clan of Scotland, await in front of the MacArthur Memorial the signal to take their place in the twenty-fifth annual Azalea Festival parade on April 25, 1981. Photograph by Carroll Walker

John Murray, fourth Earl of Dunmore, has been generally credited with ordering the bombardment of Norfolk on January 1, 1776, which subsequently resulted in its destruction. That he ordered the bombardment there is no doubt, but that he totally destroyed the town is open to question by many. It would appear that the local troops, taking advantage of the confusion generated by the bombardment and having an intense dislike of the king's sympathizers, wantonly destroyed their property; and when it was decided to evacuate the town to keep the British from returning and using it as a base, the militia destroyed what was left. Of course, it could be pointed out that Lord Dunmore's initial action precipitated the final destruction.

Be that as it may, and in a spirit of good humor (which Dunmore lacked, so the story goes), the City of Norfolk decided to let bygones be bygones and absolve him of all blame. Therefore, at the dedication of the Dunmore Docks on April 4, 1981, Mayor Vincent J. Thomas, honored Lady Anne Dunmore, the widow of the ninth Earl of Dunmore, with a plaque containing the mayor's proclamation, and making her an honorary citizen of Norfolk. Lady Dunmore graciously accepted and good-naturedly quipped," It was nice to know we got this straightened out." Photograph by Carroll Walker

Birgette N. Borch of Denmark waits on her Viking ship float for the start of the parade of the twenty-fifth annual Azalea Festival, April 25, 1981. She became Queen Azalea that after noon. Photograph by Carroll Walker

Several years ago Old Dominion University organized an International Festival to introduce Norfolkians to the customs, arts, crafts, and cuisine of many countries. Interest in the festival has grown not only through the university but also throughout the community. Forty-nine countries are represented at Old Dominion University, and the International Festival celebrates the cosmopolitan population.

This Indian dancer was photographed at the festival in March 1981. Photograph by Carroll Walker

Nigerian native costumes at the March 1981 International Festival. Photograph by Carroll Walker

At the Japanese booth visitors could buy origami paper and other Japanese articles. Photograph by Carroll Walker

Scottish sword dancers cut a fine figure at the festival. Photograph by Carroll Walker

Cuban-Spanish Dancers in a colorful rhythm. Photograph by Carroll Walker

In 1920 three music lovers in Norfolk, Marian Carpenter Miles, Dr. Robert Whitehead, and Walter E. Howe, began to organize an orchestra devoted to classical music. In short time they assembled a dozen amateur and professional players. With some support from the city, they were able to use a room in the old Armory building for rehearsals and the Armory auditorium for performances. The city council later appropriated some money for music and instruments. On April 12, 1921, the orchestra, numbering forty-three players, gave its first concert. Mr. Howe conducted, Mrs. Miles was concertmaster, and Dr. Whitehead was business manager. In later years Dr. Whitehead's son, Henry Cowles Whitehead, was conductor of the orchestra until his death at the age of thirty-eight.

In 1948 Edgar Schenkman, a graduate of the Julliard School of Music, became the symphony's conductor and guided the orchestra, now numbering seventy-five from advanced amateurs to professionals who won recognition throughout the state and participated in the Virginia Festival of Music in 1949.

Russell Stanger, composer as well as conductor, came to Norfolk in 1966 from Minneapolis, Minnesota and left in 1980.

The Norfolk Symphony Orchestra has come a long way from its formation in 1920 to its present professionalism as the Virginia Philharmonic with a new conductor, Richard Williams. The orchestra performs at Chrysler Hall—shown in the inset along with the reflecting pool. Courtesy of Virginia Philharmonic

One might have noticed him—a tall, sort of heavy-set man with a black mustache and beard, invariably wearing a black Greek fisherman's cap—somewhere along Mowbray Arch or on a shady street in Ghent, stopping to sketch or scribble something in a notebook; and sometimes, with a camera in hand he may have paused in front of some seemingly insignificant object to take a picture. If ever you saw such a man, you were undoubtedly looking at A. B. Jackson, Jr., a widely acclaimed Norfolk artist who lived in Ghent and taught at Old Dominion University. Regrettably, he will no longer be a part of the local scene, for he passed away the week of March 23, 1981.

From New Haven, Connecticut, and son of a railroad man, Jackson worked his way through school as a station redcap. His work won many awards and was exhibited at many museums and galleries in the East: the Virginia Museum, Chrysler Museum, Yale University, and Old Dominion University. The private collection of Mrs. Lyndon B. Johnson contains some of Jackson's work.

In 1967 Jackson became the first full-time black faculty member of Old Dominion University. His series of paintings of people who sat in the half shadows of their front porches, watching the world go by, he called "Porch People." Later he published a book of photographs and paintings entitled As I See Ghent: A Visual Essay in which he captured the sparkle of water through a bridge railing, a geometrical pattern formed by lines of a sidewalk, and many other details of Ghent that hardly anyone seemed to notice.

One of Jackson's little sketches shows twelve heads of many different people he saw from time to time in the Ghent area; it appeared in his Ghent book. One of his paintings entitled "Chamber" is also shown here, but black and white can't convey the warm feeling that flows from the reds, browns, and yellows in the original.

A local critic and artist expressed the feelings of many people: "I think his death will be quite a blow to the whole Virginia arts scene—not just Norfolk and Tidewater." Courtesy of The Donning Company/Publishers

215

Kenneth Harris was born in Pennsylvania in 1904, reared in the South and moved to Norfolk in 1949. In 1950, he was commissioned by the Norfolk (now Chrysler) Museum to do a series of thirty watercolors of Norfolk as it was then. The collection, called "Portrait of a City," was shown in more than twenty-five museums and galleries throughout the South. He has done over five hundred watercolors for Colonial Williamsburg, under an arrangement with the Restoration, and twenty watercolors for the Rockefeller estate.

One of the most popular and beloved painters in Tidewater, Kenneth Harris is also known for his fine essays, and has published two books, How To Make A Living As A Painter (1954) and The Necessity for Nonconformity (1976).

In 1979 the Virginia Stage Company, a resident professional theatrical company, acquired the old Wells Theatre on Tazewell Street for the purpose of producing original professional quality plays as well as revivals of established plays. The Wells is Norfolk's oldest operating theatre, having opened on August 26, 1913, with the musical comedy The Merry Countess. Over the years many famous stars have appeared on its stage, such as Anna Held, John Drew, Robert B. Mantell, and Will Rogers. Maude Adams appeared in Peter Pan in 1913 and later that year Ben Hur came to the Wells with a cast of 200. Vaudeville played there for awhile, and although movies were shown in the 1920s, stage shows came back from time to time, the last, perhaps, being the D'Oyle Carte Players in their repertoire of Gilbert and Sullivan in the early 1930s. This photograph was taken in 1913. Courtesy of Virginia Stage Company

Harborfest-1980

When the United States celebrated its bicentennial in 1976, Norfolk participated with Operation Sail—a program of events along the waterfront which included water skiing, boat racing, underwater demolition maneuvers, and the visit of the tall ships. The Danish training ship Danmark, a beautiful full-rigged ship, was the most outstanding guest but no stranger to these parts, having first visited Norfolk in 1935.

The success of Operation Sail generated a similar event in 1977, and thus Harborfest—now an annual tradition—was launched.

Harborfest-1980 was especially exciting. Sailing ships from eight countries raced to Norfolk from Cartagena, Colombia. On the morning of May 21, beneath dark, heavy clouds, an array of ships of all types assembled off Fort Wool and, led by Jacques Cousteau in the Calypso, proceeded up the Elizabeth River to the downtown waterfront. Such a spectacular parade of sail never had been witnessed here before, except possibly at the Jamestown Exposition in 1907.

Festivities began Thursday morning, May 22, when the tall ships opened for visitors. Along the waterfront a variety of refreshment stands, souvenir booths, and bands—some from Jamaica, the Bahamas, Trinidad, and Tobago—entertained visitors.

On Saturday afternoon there was a blessing of the boats as many of the smaller craft left to race to Boston for that city's tricentennial festival. A fireworks display was postponed from Saturday night to Sunday night becaue of sudden rain; however, spirits were not dampened: all day Sunday people crowded to the waterfront for the Norfolk Symphony Orchestra's concert under the stars on Towne Point and a dazzling fireworks display.

It was estimated that more than 200,000 people attended the festivities that last evening. Ever the politician, Mayor Vince Thomas wistfully remarked from an observation point high in the Omni Hotel: "If we could only get that many people out on election day."

Under a cloudy sky, the tall ships are shown rounding the Naval Base, led by two Navy tugs (only one of which is shown here), on their way up the Elizabeth River to Norfolk to begin Harborfest-1980. The Ecaudoran square-rigger Guayas is on the left. The Spanish four-masted topsail schooner Juan Sebastian de Elcano is the largest of the ships. The two ships on the right are The Pride of Baltimore and the Unicorn. Photograph by Carroll Walker

217

Like moths fluttering about, small sailing craft escort the Juan Sebastian de Elcano, *Spanish naval cadet training ship, to her berth in downtown Norfolk. Photograph by S. H. Ringo, 1980*

The square-rigged Guayas nears her berth on the downtown waterfront. Photograph by S. H. Ringo

The race of a number of tall ships to Norfolk from Cartegena, Colombia, was arranged by the Sail Training Association of England the American Sail Training Association of Newport, Rhode Island. The winner was the cadet naval training ship Gloria of Colombia, followed by the Guayas of Ecuador and the Juan Sebastian de Elcano of Spain, also naval cadet training ships. The first two ships were bark-rigged sailing ships and the Spanish ship a four-masted topsail schooner. Other ships also participated in the race.

The cadets and members of these and other early arriving ships lined up at City Hall. Photograph by Carroll Walker

Representative William G. Whitehurst presents the award to the captain of the Gloria winner in the race from Cartegena. Mayor Vincent J. Thomas looks on. Photograph by Carroll Walker

It has been many decades since square-rigged ships docked at Norfolk's waterfront. In the picture are the Gloria of Colombia and the Guayas of Ecuador. Photograph by Carroll Walker

Crowds visit the three square-riggers, the Unicorn United States, the Guayas (Ecuador), and the Gloria (Colombia) on Norfolk's downtown waterfront. Photograph by Carroll Walker

Cadets and crew members of the Colombian square-rigger Gloria take positions on the yards in a farewell salute to Norfolk. Photograph by Carroll Walker

With Waterfront Drive closed to vehicular traffic, crowds fill the thoroughfare to watch the fireworks display that closes Harborfest-1980. Photograph by Carroll Walker

Fireworks light up the sky as Harborfest-1980 comes to an end. The lights of Portsmouth are in the distance. Photograph by Carroll Walker

Many changes have taken place in Norfolk's waterfront skyline since Benjamin Henry Latrobe made his skyline sketch of Norfolk in 1796. In this 1981 picture the Virginia National Bank and the Omni International Hotel dominate the downtown waterfront area. Ferries once docked where a part of the hotel is located. Photograph by Carroll Walker

As an energy crisis spreads throughout the world, nations seek alternatives to oil. Because of its vast reserves of coal, they have turned to the United States, and their colliers head for Hampton Roads. Because the coal companies were unable to fill orders promptly, ships have had to wait days, even weeks, before getting a berth at the piers. At one time it was estimated that over 150 ships lay at anchor in the area. This photo shows colliers waiting for a berth. Photograph by Mort Fryman, 1981

Norfolk's skyline of 1907. The area covered in the picture is from the old Y.M.C.A. building (left), a site now occupied by the Citizens Office Building, built 1899, to Church Street (extreme right). The tall building is the National Bank of Commerce Building, now First and Merchants National Bank Building, built 1905. Courtesy of Kirn Memorial Library

Through the sand hills and wind-blown sea oats of Cape Henry, a favorite spot of Harry C. Mann, this picture was taken of a four-masted schooner sailing southward under a heavy sky, laden with a full cargo for some foreign port. Many more such ships would follow. It is small wonder, then, that Norfolk should have on its seal the outline of a sailing ship to represent ships of all ages that have visited its harbor since 1680, bringing both destruction and pestilence, prosperity and wealth. Photograph by Harry C. Mann, 1910; courtesy of Kirn Memorial Library

Bibliography

Many sources have been consulted in researching data for the pictures and text in this book, such as the records of the Circuit Court of the City of Chesapeake, Virginia, for Norfolk County, and records of the Corporation Court of the City of Norfolk as well as the city Survey Office.

The microfilm files of Norfolk newspapers going back to the late eighteenth century on file in the Sargeant Room of the Kirn Memorial Library have been used extensively as well as other printed sources, such as early borough and city directories dating from 1801 up to the present date.

In addition to many printed sources in my possession, there were others in the collection of the Sargeant Memorial Room of the Kirn Memorial Library, including maps.

Burton, Harrison W. *History of Norfolk, Va.* Norfolk, 1877.

Calendar of Virginia State Papers and other Manuscripts, 1652-1869. Richmond, Va., 1875-1893. 11 vols.

Chambers, Lenoir, and Joseph E. Shank. *Salt Walter and Printer's Ink: A History of Norfolk and Its Newspapers—1865-1955.* Chapel Hill, N. C., 1967.

Forrest, William S. *Historical and Descriptive Sketches of Norfolk and Vicinity.* Philadelphia, Pa., 1853.

Historical Sketch of the Volunteers of Norfolk and Portsmouth, Va. Brief histories of the local militia companies. Norfolk, Va., 1898.

Lamb, Robert W. *Our Twin Cities.* Norfolk, Va., 1887-8.

Porter, John W. H. *History of Norfolk County, Virginia: 1861-65.* A history of events in Norfolk and Norfolk County and men and organizations of the area who served in the Confederate States Army or Navy. Portsmouth, Va., 1892.

de St. Mery, Moreau. *American Journey, 1793-1798: Kenneth Roberts and Anna M. Roberts.* A visit to Norfolk, 1793. Garden City, N. Y., 1947.

Squires, W. H. T. Scrapbooks in Sargeant Room, Kirn Memorial Library. Norfolk history published in the Norfolk *Ledger-Dispatch,* 1935-48.

Stewart, William H. *A History of Norfolk County, Virginia, and Representative Citizens.* Chicago, Ill., 1902.

Rowland, Thomas B. Scrapbooks in Sargeant Memorial Room, Kirn Memorial Library. Notes and newspaper clippings from colonial days to 1912.

Tucker, George H. *Norfolk Highlights, 1584-1881.* A collection of stories of Norfolk's past. Norfolk, 1972.

Whichard, Rogers Dey. *History of Lower Tidewater Virginia.* New York, N. Y., 1959.

Wertenbaker, Thomas Jefferson. *Norfolk: Historic Southern Port.* Durham, N. C., 1931. Second edition, edited by Marvin W. Schlegel, 1962.

Index

About the author:

Carroll H. Walker attended local public schools, and worked for Norfolk & Western Railway Company for thirty-eight years. he studied art at the New York School of Industrial Art, was a Spanish interpreter on passenger steamers to South America and first took free-lance photography in 1937. Mr. Walker has a collection of over 500 original prints of military uniforms in the U. S., over 1,000 military minatures of soldiers in uniform (which he paints himself), and has been collecting photos on the city of Norfolk for over forty years. He is a Fellow of The Company of Military Historians in Washington, D. C., served on the Civil War Centennial Commission, and is now a member of the Norfolk Tricentennial Commission. He has been a member of the Junior Chamber of Commerce, the Sons of Confederate Veterans, and is presently a director of the Norfolk Historical Society. His column, "Those Were the Days," ran for seven years in the Sunday edition of The Virginian-Pilot. He lives in Norfolk with his wife Isabella, has a son, Carroll H. (Skip) Walker, Jr., a resident of New York, and a daughter, Carroll Teresa Walker, who resides in Washington, D. C.